Telling Your Story

PRESERVE YOUR HISTORY THROUGH STORYTELLING

Jerry Apps

T0169031

FULCRUM

Library of Congress Cataloging-in-Publication Data

Names: Apps, Jerold W., 1934- author.
Title: Telling your story / by Jerry Apps.
Description: Golden, CO : Fulcrum Publishing, 2016.
Identifiers: LCCN 2016019291 | ISBN 9781938486234 (paperback)
Subjects: LCSH: Autobiography--Authorship. | Biography as a literary form. |
  BISAC: LANGUAGE ARTS & DISCIPLINES / Composition & Creative Writing.
Classification: LCC CT25 .A66 2016 | DDC 808/.06692--dc23
LC record available at https://lccn.loc.gov/2016019291
978-1-938486-23-4

Printed in the United States.

Fulcrum Publishing
4690 Table Mountain Drive, Suite 100
Golden, Colorado 80403
(800) 992-2908 • (303) 277-1623
www.fulcrumbooks.com

CONTENTS

Introduction

Each of us has a story to tell. We may not be comfortable telling it or lack the skill to do it easily, but nonetheless the story is there. Our stories make us human, and it is through our stories that we communicate who we are to others. We each have at least three kinds of stories to tell—those that come from within us and offer a window to our personal being, those that are about our relationships with others, and finally those stories that are about our connection to the world around us. Psychologist Adam Alter describes these three kinds of stories as three worlds, "… the world within us, the world between us, and the world around us…"[1]

On these pages I discuss how important storytelling has been for me, from when I was a boy growing up on a farm, in high school when I was editor of my school newspaper, during the years when I taught at the University of Wisconsin–Madison, to now, when I work as a full time writer, creative writing teacher, and storyteller. I share my storytelling journey on these pages—and at the same time I share tips, suggestions, and pitfalls to avoid for others who want to tell their stories.

In this book I focus on the personal story. I explain how to create it and how to share it through writing, personal appearances, and using radio and television. There is great joy in unearthing one's personal story, but there can be even greater joy in sharing it—thus my emphasis on both writing and sharing stories.

At one time, telling one's stories was viewed as a project for the elderly—and certainly one is never too old to share a story. But as Natalie Goldberg writes, "…people are disclosing their lives in their twenties, writing their first memoir in their thirties, and their second in their forties. This revolution in personal narrative that has unrolled across the American landscape in the last two and a half decades is the expression of a uniquely American energy: a desire to understand in the heat of living, while life is fresh, and not wait til old age—it may be too late."[2] From young to old, people are telling their stories—and many more could.

PART I

Your Story

1
Why Tell Your Story?

My father and my uncles were storytellers, and so were several of the neighbors in the farming community where I grew up in central Wisconsin. Family members told stories when we gathered for celebrations, birthday parties, anniversaries, and at Christmas and Thanksgiving family affairs. Our farm neighbors told stories during threshing and wood sawing bees, while they waited at the grist mill for their cow feed to be ground, and when they came to town on Saturday nights and waited for their wives to grocery shop. These stories were always entertaining, as many of them had a humorous bent to them, but they also were filled with information—how the cattle were surviving during the summer drought, what price Sam got for his potato crop and how he managed to get that price. How the weather this year was not nearly as bad as the weather twenty years ago. Many of the stories were also sad, such as how Frank was making it on his poor farm since his wife died and left him with three kids to feed and care for.

I heard some of these stories many times, each told a little differently when it was shared, but enjoyed as much as the time before. When I graduated from college in 1955, I began a long career as a teacher. I was soon telling stories as a teaching method. As the years passed, I discovered how much I enjoyed telling my stories, both in written form and spoken in front of an audience. I also discovered that people enjoyed my stories when I shared them on radio and television.

In 1999, I was in New York City as part of an international group discussing the arts for people over age 50. The week-long session, sponsored by the American Association of Retired Persons (AARP) and UNESCO, the educational arm of the United Nations, focused on developing suggestions for how middle-aged people and older could become more involved in the arts, and how they and the world might benefit from them doing so. We discussed sculpting and painting, dance and folk arts—and storytelling. I was in the storytelling group, and we discussed and made several suggestions about the importance of storytelling and how to encourage people to do it.

Each sub-group was asked to select a spokesperson who would present the group's report to the United Nation's delegates at the end of the week. I was selected to give the storytelling group's report and I never forgot the experience. Here I was, at the podium in the beautiful United Nations building, looking out over a sea of delegates, many wearing headphones that provided them with a translation to their own language of what I had to say. Sitting close behind me was Kofi Annan, then Secretary General of the UN. I had fifteen minutes to deliver my message.

I don't recall the exact words I used, but I tried to convey that storytelling and stories were as old as humankind and that they remained important and could make many valuable contributions. I couldn't tell by looking at the audience if they agreed with me, disagreed with me, or just didn't care. When I finished—mine was the last in a series of brief talks about the arts—I left the podium and stepped off to the side. I noticed that several delegates had lined up to talk with me. I expected to hear such things as: "You were talking about an earlier day when people had time to share stories. Today the events of the world move too rapidly for storytelling." I expected someone to say, "Today's world requires more modern ways of communicating, and storytelling ought to be relegated to history."

But that's not what I heard. The first person thanked me for sharing the importance of storytelling, as did the second, who went on to say that it was as important today as it has ever been, perhaps even more so.

But what the third person said has stayed with me most clearly. A woman from an African country that I can't remember looked me right in the eye and said, "In my country, we have known the power of stories for generations; we know their importance and we encourage their telling." Continuing without a hint of a smile, she said, "You people have allowed others to tell your story. You've allowed novels, TV, and the movies to tell your story."

I didn't know how to respond, for at that moment with the words "you people," I apparently represented everyone in the United States. I didn't know how to respond because I knew she was right. We have become enamored with the stories on TV, in the films that we see, and the novels that we read. We have come to believe that our individual stories and their telling no longer matter—that they somehow are irrelevant in the larger scheme of things.

By 1999, I had been involved for nearly 30 years in teaching writing workshops designed to help people get in touch with and write their own stories. I had also published several books that included my personal stories. When I taught graduate courses at the University of Wisconsin–Madison, I regularly used storytelling as part of my teaching approach. But during my last several years of teaching at the university, I had come to doubt the importance of stories and storytelling. In fact, one of my university colleagues told me, "Students these days don't have time for stories—they want the information they need to succeed in their fields as efficiently and quickly as possible. There is no time for storytelling." Another colleague was even more blunt. He said, "Apps, if you didn't spend so much time writing and telling stories, you might amount to something."

This is why what the African UN delegate said to me resonated so strongly. She affirmed what I already knew: that stories and storytelling were important, and that we in the United States have indeed allowed others to tell our stories. From that day on, I never wavered in my zeal for writing and telling stories, and helping others write their stories. I have long known how important stories are to me, to my family, and for those who live in my community. Through my writing workshops, I have seen the power of stories and storytelling come alive in front of me as participants wrote their stories and shared them.

Now my challenge became how to encourage others to tell their stories. One way to do this was to help people see what telling their individual stories could accomplish, and why personal stories can be one of the most valuable things a person possesses. Nancy Lamb said it well when she wrote, "I believe we look to story for a connection to our past. Story reaches beyond the written word to create an unconscious continuity with our earliest ancestors, as well as with future generations …in making these connections, we honor where we came from, who we are, and what we can become."[3]

I tell the students who attend my life story writing workshops, "We are our histories." I point out that when we tell our stories we can begin to understand who we are.

Recently, I completed two hour-long documentaries for public television in which I told stories about what farm life was like during the latter years of the Depression and through World War II. These were my stories of life on a central Wisconsin farm during a time when electricity had not yet come to the country, when we milked cows by hand, heated our farmhouse with wood stoves, and I attended a one-room country school with one teacher and all eight grades in one room.

After the programs aired, I received stories from people with similar experiences from all around the country and many from Canada as well. It seemed by telling my stories, it gave permission for others to tell theirs.

The benefits of storytelling are many. Families benefit as stories tie generations together. Communities also benefit, for as community members share their personal stories and their histories, a community can began to understand itself. The historical record benefits because the stories told by ordinary people add a depth and breadth to history that goes beyond what the professional historians are able to accomplish. The stories of ordinary people entertain, they inform, and they can influence as well. As new challenges appear and new problems emerge, revisiting the stories of a community can often offer insight to those making decisions about future directions. There is some truth to what philosopher George Santayana said: "Those who do not remember the past are condemned to repeat it."

The Importance of Stories

In our hurry-up, highly technological society, which too often appears to be controlled by electronic devices that send terse little messages with invented words, we overlook the importance of stories. Why are stories important?

Stories help us recall the past while opening a window to the future. One of the one-liners that I share with my writing students is: "We don't know where we're going until we know where we've been." Stories tie us to our past and at the same time provide a platform for facing the future.

Stories evoke feelings and deeper thoughts. Stories usually include facts about an event or a memory we may hold, but by weaving the facts into a story we touch feelings and move ourselves to think more deeply about what we are reading or hearing, especially as it relates to our own lives.

My family has a great storytelling tradition. Whenever we get together, stories become a part of the conversation. I tell stories. My children tell stories that have been passed on from my grandfather, to my father, to me, to my children, and now to my grandchildren.

By sharing our stories, we are coming out from behind ourselves. We are letting other people know a little more of who we are. By telling stories, we also let ourselves know a little more about who we are.

Storytelling can take us to a place within ourselves where we have never been. It can change us forever. Those are powerful words, but I've seen this happen again and again as I have worked with more than 1,000 writing students over the past 40 years. And it has happened to me personally several times as I have examined the life I've lived and have written stories about it.

Our stories can help us discover meaning in our lives without defining or describing it. As we write our personal stories, we often discover meaning that defies definition and description. This newly discovered meaning may be difficult to put into words, yet it may have a profound effect on us personally.

Stories help make us human; when we forget our stories, we forget who we are. Stories ground us, give us pleasure, and provide a sense of purpose in our lives.

Stories are the history of a civilization. They chronicle the history of families, farms, villages, and cities. These stories stitched together form the history of who we are as a people.

I discovered long ago that one of the best ways to learn, and often the easiest, is with a story. As a longtime teacher, I tell stories to make a point. I often hear from my former students who will share a story that I told and tell me how they have never forgotten the point that it made. Remembering a story is usually far easier than memorizing a list of dates, names, and places that so many students are asked to memorize. Put these dates, names, and places in a story and the message comes alive; the information is now in context with relevance and meaning.

The mental pictures in the stories we tell are often far better than those we see on television or in the movies. As a kid I listened to radio programs: *The Lone Ranger, Terry and the Pirates, Captain Midnight, Jack Armstrong,* and others. I listened on a battery-operated radio as we had no electricity on the farm. But listen I did and in my mind I formed vivid pictures of exactly what was happening. The stories tapped into my imagination and I lived them right along with the radio actors who were telling them. I saw the pictures in my mind as clearly as if they were printed on paper.

By sharing our stories, we come out from behind ourselves. We let other people know a little more about who we are. We also let *ourselves* know more about who we are. Storytelling can take us to a place within ourselves where we have never been and can change us forever.

I've seen this happen again and again as I've worked with more than a thousand writing students over the past forty years. And it has happened to me several times as I have examined the life I've lived and written stories about it.

Personal Benefits of Storytelling

A dozen or so years ago, a man named Charlie enrolled in my week-long writing workshop at The Clearing. The Clearing, in northern Door County, Wisconsin, is a residential adult learning center devoted to the arts and humanities, with classes ranging from writing to woodcarving, from quilting to music appreciation, and from painting to nature study.

Charlie did not want to be in my workshop; it was his son's idea and his son even paid his fees to attend. Charlie, in his late 70s at the time, was a World War II veteran. He had served in Okinawa and had told no one about his war experiences, not even his wife. He had no intention of telling anyone. Yet, that was the reason his son paid his way to the writing workshop, for Charlie's son wanted his twin sons, Charlie's grandsons, to know what Charlie had experienced during the war.

Charlie was slim and rather soft spoken, and had a wry sense of humor. He was friendly to everyone, except when the topic of WWII came up. Then he simply clammed up and refused to talk about it.

On the first day of the workshop, when I asked participants to say a word or two about who they were, where they were from, and what they hoped to gain from the week, Charlie muttered something about how his family wanted him to write some of his war experiences. From the look on Charlie's face, it was clear he wished he were anywhere else but in this writing workshop. Charlie's wife, Jean, attended the workshop with him. She said she had wanted to write something about how she and Charlie had first met, but said nothing about Charlie's assignment from his son.

That first day, the group met two hours in the morning and another two hours in the afternoon. Charlie said little. He sat there, looking very uncomfortable.

On the second day, Charlie asked if he could meet with me privately, an offer I had extended to everyone in the workshop. That afternoon, when the formal workshop session ended, I sat with a very glum-looking Charlie. He said to me, "You know I'm supposed to be writing my war stories while I'm here, don't you?"

"Yes, I know that," I said. Jean had told me privately about what their son had done.

"Well, I just don't know where to start—it's a long, terrible story."

I asked him where he had served, and he said "Okinawa. And it was awful."

Then he began telling me the story of his unit's landing on that Japanese-controlled island. As he talked, the tears began running down his face as the horrid memories of April 1945 came flooding back in vivid detail. He talked for an hour, nearly nonstop. I listened. He stopped when it was time for supper, and before we parted, I said he should write down what he had just told me.

"Nobody wants to know about all of this," Charlie said.

"Your family wants to know," I said quietly. And so Charlie began writing and, outside of the time he spent in class and at meals, he wrote constantly that week. He eventually published a book, *The Battle of Okinawa: My Experience, The Last Battle of World War II*. He began his book with these words:

> *At 0300 hours we were awakened in our quarters below deck by Captain Haddo, who announced we were disembarking at 0600 hours into enemy territory, specifically the island of Okinawa.*

We had been briefed by our officers only the day before as to our destination. For weeks we thought it was going to be the southern beaches of Japan.

Charlie went on to share in vivid detail the awfulness of war, the heroics of some, and the plain luck of others who survived without a physical scratch but with emotional wounds that lasted a lifetime. As the workshop week progressed, I could see a change in Charlie as these pent-up memories spilled out on paper and were shared orally with other workshop participants. He was smiling more; the sullen expression of the first days in class had disappeared. Charlie's story is but one of many that I heard from veterans who had clammed up when they returned home from war.

In the 25 years I have taught writing workshops at The Clearing, there are many similar tales. During one workshop, I noticed a woman, who I guessed to be in her thirties, walking with a cane and a bit unsteady on her feet. On the first day of class, when I asked what participants wanted to accomplish during the week, this young woman's statement caught everyone by surprise. Very quietly she said, "I have brain cancer and less than a year to live. I'm here to write my stories so my children don't forget their mother." The room was filled with silence. For a few long moments no one said anything. I gathered up enough gumption to say, "We're all here to help you in any way we can." And we did. By week's end, she had written several of her stories, and she left the workshop with a smile on her face. I assured her that her children would never forget her. The participants in the workshop that week surely didn't.

Other workshop students have shared stories of childhood abuse, of growing up in poverty, of having abusive spouses, of surviving the death of a child or a close friend or a parent. Or they have had a devastating disease that turned their lives completely around—and for whatever reason these people had chosen to keep the story inside, to keep the experience locked up in their memories. I was one of them.

In January of 1947 I came down with polio. My right knee was paralyzed for six months. I couldn't walk, couldn't do much of anything during that time. That fall I entered high school and, although by then I could walk, I couldn't run and thus could not play baseball or basketball, or do all the other things my classmates were able to do. I was a miserable kid who felt absolutely worthless. Several teachers came to my aid—they pushed me in other directions, such as into public speaking and into writing.

When I went off to college, I wanted no one to know about my polio experience. These were the days of the Korean War. I passed an Army physical; the doctor didn't ask me if I had had polio, which surely would have exempted me from military service. I had only a slight limp by that time, and I could do most of what was required of me without too much difficulty.

After serving in the military, I interviewed for and landed a job with the University of Wisconsin Agricultural Extension. I found I was able to do the work, but was constantly worried that I couldn't do it well enough because, as I think back now, the feelings of worthlessness and inadequacy that I had acquired when I had polio remained with me. It was only recently that I began sharing my polio story. I felt better about doing it, and soon I was hearing from other polio survivors, each with a story to tell.

Preserving Your Stories

Your stories are snippets of history. They deserve to be preserved and made available for others to read. Many students in my writing classes are writing their stories to share with their family and close friends. One personal story writer included one of his growing up stories with the Christmas letter he sent each year. Some of my students include their stories in blogs that they write for the Internet. Several of my students have collected their stories, made sure they were well edited, and then made multiple copies of them in a simple book form that was produced at a local copy shop or office supply store.

In addition to their families and close friends, I encourage my students to share copies of their stories with their local historical society and with their public library.

A few of my writing students choose to distribute their stories more widely through various publishing means. Today there are many alternatives for both self-publishing and traditional publishing. Go to the Internet and type in "Publishing Opportunities" to see a long list of what is available. However, a word of caution concerning some publishing firms catering to self-publishing authors: Some firms may be more interested in your money than in doing a good job of publishing and promoting your work.

2

What Is a Story?

The word *story* is widely used in our society's vocabulary. For purposes of this book, I have a very specific and traditional definition. Before I explain, here are a few ways that the word *story* is used in everyday life:

- **To depict gossip:** "There are a lot of stories going around about that person."

- **As a lie:** "Mable stays with the truth; she never tells a story." When we share information with another person, the reply we sometimes get is "That's just a story isn't it?" suggesting that stories are not true, but merely fabrications or a product of someone's imagination. Indeed "short stories" as a genre are fiction; they are made up stories, which further confuses the issue.

- **As a report of an event:** "The evening TV news carried several stories about the recent flood." A news story is not a story in the traditional sense but a report of something that has happened, and unfortunately, it often involves a report of a violent occurrence—a car wreck, plane crash, fire, terrorist bombing, and such. Occasionally the media will run a traditional story about someone, but when they do, they will call it a feature story. What the media calls a story is usually a report, and when they run a traditional story, they call it something else. No wonder people are confused about what is a story, in the traditional sense of the meaning.

- **Background information about something or someone:** "What's the story behind Fred's arrest?" What people are really looking for when they ask this question are the facts of the situation. What did Fred do that prompted his arrest? If they dig deeply enough, and ask a few questions, they may find a story there as well—something that goes considerably deeper than merely information.

- **When someone doesn't want to expand on an explanation:** "Of course, that's another story." Someone may begin explaining something and then stop and proclaim, "That's another story," which likely means they have an alternative explanation of a situation that they don't wish to share.

- **When shortening up a long explanation of something.** "To make a long story short, I fired the guy." Sometimes, when explaining something, a person will start with, "To make a long story short." What the person means is that he will give a shortened version of something he has seen, something he has done, some situation he has encountered. What he is doing is not sharing a story, but is describing something—in shortened form.

We use the word *story* when we don't want to expand on something we've just explained ("Well, that's a another story."), when we have nothing more to add ("And that's the end of that story."), and when describing something that happens frequently ("It's the same old story.").

As you can see, *story* is a hardworking word. But for the purposes of this book, I define *story* as your personal story.

What Is a Personal Story?

A personal story is true—not a product of someone's imagination. Novelists write stories, and the techniques they use and the product that evolves from their work is a story, but not a true story. I also write novels and find the techniques and writing approaches I use for fiction helpful in writing my personal stories.

The stories I am talking about here are recounts of occurrences that have happened in a real person's life. They usually include a series of events, enhanced with details, and made colorful with dialogue, and that ultimately have meaning for the writer. I encourage you to write the stories that go deeper than merely recounting events. Your stories are a reflection of who you are and have special meaning for you. Ultimately you may touch those who read/hear your stories in a profound way as well.

Stories have a beginning, a middle, and an end. But they include more than that. As writer and editor Phillip Martin says, "A story goes somewhere. It follows, with purpose, one or more characters through a series of events. By the end it arrives at a target destination, fulfilling its reason for being told."[4]

The main character in most of your personal stories will be you, the writer. As you tell your stories, take us, the readers, beyond what happened, to the meaning of what happened. One of the great mysteries and joys of telling your story is that meaning may emerge. You may have experienced something many years ago, such as losing your job or going through a divorce. You remember the details of the event well, but you probably have not thought much about the meaning of it—until you begin writing the story. In the story I shared about Charlie, the World War II veteran, the meaning of surviving a horrendous situation emerged as he wrote the story and shared it. The circumstances of the event had obviously nagged at him for years, and once he wrote about the event in all its gory detail, he began to realize the meaning of the event and felt a great burden lift from his shoulders.

I encourage you to write stories that go deeper than merely recounting events. Your stories are a reflection of who you are and have special meaning for you. Ultimately your stories may be profoundly moving to those who read or hear them, as well.

3

Ways to Tell Stories

Even within the category of "personal stories," there are many ways to tell about our own lives and experiences.

You might have heard the terms *reminiscence, autobiography*, and *memoir*. What do they mean, and how do they relate to your story? You've likely heard these terms tossed around in writing classes you've attended, or perhaps a friend inquired about what you are doing these days, and you respond that you're writing your life stories. The friend may reply, "Oh, you're working on your autobiography." Or the friend may ask if you're working on your memoir or perhaps she may wonder if you're writing personal reminiscences.

Knowing the differences among these various forms of life story can help keep you focused, and ultimately result in a better outcome. Stories can and often are triggered by reminiscences, and stories are generally an integral part of autobiographies and memoirs. Let's look a little more deeply at these relationships.

Reminiscence

Your personal story begins with your memories—your reminiscences of events that have occurred in your life. But merely recounting a memory is not sharing a story. For example, I attended a one-room country school for eight years. I have many memories of that experience—walking a mile back and forth to school in all kinds of weather. Arriving at the school on a cold day in winter and spending the entire day huddled around the wood-burning stove to keep warm. Walking home in a blizzard. Playing softball on a diamond where the bases were trees; a box elder was first base, a black oak was second, and a white oak was third. The end of the school year picnic.

These kinds of memories are wonderful beginning places for story writing. Indeed I have written several stories based on these memories. But by themselves they are not stories.

Autobiography

When you write your autobiography, you begin with your birth and end with the present time. You include all the incidents in your life, usually in chronological order. Your autobiography may include stories—indeed, many stories—which will help your reader appreciate and understand the life that you have lived.

The challenge in writing an autobiography (a biography is when you write about another person) is that it is an enormous task. If done well, meaning it is an in-depth account of your life so far lived, it will require more time and energy than most beginning life story writers will want to undertake.

Unfortunately, some life story writers believe that telling their story means telling the entire story of their lives thus far. That telling their story means telling the entire story of their lives up to the present day.

A few years ago, one of my life story writing students turned in a manuscript that he titled, "My Story." He began writing that he was born in Indianapolis, Indiana—he gave the date and year. He went on to write, "I was born in the midst of the Great Depression. My childhood was quite normal, even though we didn't have much beyond the necessities. I attended grade school in Indianapolis. We moved to Minnesota after my father lost his job in Indiana. His new job was in Minneapolis. Things got better when World War II began and jobs became more plentiful."

Then he wrote that he graduated from high school, spent two years serving in the army in Korea, got married when he returned home, raised a family of four, and had decent jobs in the Twin Cities area. He finished his "autobiography" by writing that he was now retired and enjoying his grandchildren.

In truth, we learn little about this man's life, only the briefest sketch of the life he has led so far. We want to hear the stories—what it was like being a kid during the Great Depression; the sights, smells, and sounds; the feelings he had during that time. We want to know what it was like to move to another state. What it was like in Korea and what his role was there. And so on. The hints for great stories are there, but only the hints.

My advice to beginning life story writers is to not work on an autobiography, but to concentrate on writing memoirs.

Memoir

A memoir focuses on one aspect of your life. It does not attempt to include everything. As a memoirist, you select special events and people to write/talk about. Writer William Zinsser said it well: "The problem is that an interesting life doesn't make an interesting memoir. Only small pieces of a life make an interesting memoir." [5]

In telling your story, select incidents, events, and people that help your audience learn a bit more about you and what made a difference in your life. Some of the events may be major; others may seem small and insignificant, but if they had special meaning for you, by all means consider including them.

Here is an example of something I remember:

I was eleven years old on August 14, 1945. My brothers, dad, mother, and I were attending the regular outdoor free movies held every Tuesday evening in Wild Rose, Wisconsin. The movie had just begun when we heard gun shots and, looking around, saw a parade of soldiers marching down Main Street—old soldiers, I learned later, who had fought in World War I. They were shooting and shouting, "The war is over! The war is over! It's V–J Day. Japan has surrendered. Our boys are coming home."

Soon everyone was on Main Street. The movie went on, but no one was watching. Everyone was celebrating the end of World War II. People were hugging and cheering and jumping up and down. But not everyone. I saw a woman standing off to the side and she was crying. I asked Pa why and he said, "Because her son was killed in the war and he won't be coming home."

On that day, as an eleven year old caught up in the celebration of World War II ending, I learned a little bit about the horrors of war, and that people die while fighting, and not everyone has something to celebrate.

To create this little story, I began with a simple reminiscence of what happened on that July evening and, following good storytelling practice, shaped it into a memoir with a beginning, a middle, and an end, adding detail and dialogue along the way. The line about the woman crying because her son wasn't coming home added both emotion and meaning to the story. I ended with what the event meant to me as an eleven-year-old.

PART II

Where Do Stories Come From?

4

Memories and Memory Triggers

One of the most important tools in telling personal stories is memories. Yet students in my life story writing workshops often say, "How am I supposed to remember something that happened when I was a kid when I can't remember what I had for breakfast?" I assure them that they have lots more tucked away in their memories than they imagine. I know many students, especially those who are older, don't believe me, but most are good sports and participate in a series of exercises I use to help them remember their stories. They are often surprised at how productive these simple memory triggers can be.

House Plan

I use this exercise in all of my workshops, and with few exceptions it works extremely well. Besides that, most people have fun with it. The exercise goes like this: I give each person a large piece of paper (in my workshops I provide sheets of 9 x 12" artist's sketch paper).

I ask them to draw the floor plan for the house or apartment they lived in when they were ten to twelve years old. I ask them to put the furniture in the rooms, place the pictures on the walls, and indicate which family members were most associated with each room. I ask them to jot down the smells they remember, and mention the feelings they have associated with various rooms. I give them 10 to 15 minutes to do this.

When they have finished drawing, I ask them to write a story about something that happened in one of the rooms. Here is a story one of my writing students wrote after doing the house plan exercise:

Extra Rare Steaks
by Bob Leder

Summer on the farm has its own schedule. The rigid routines of school days are gone, no bus to rush to catch. The early morning sun casts its glow over the land before one gets up for morning chores. Every day is a new opportunity to start anew, make plans, and take control of one's life, so to speak. Especially for a young school boy eager to enjoy the new freedom summer brings. This was a time of year that I truly enjoyed.

The time after chores and before breakfast was my favorite time to train calves to lead for the county fair later in the summer. The air is crisp and cool, and I had lots of energy at that time of day. On one such bright clear day, as I emerged from the barn with my 600-pound Holstein-Hereford cross steer, Curly, I discovered that my favorite aunt, Aunt Frieda, had arrived for a visit while I was still in the barn. Eager to show her my steer, I shouted out from the driveway, in an attempt to gain her attention. There was no response from within the house. So I led Curly closer to the house and called out again, still no response. Figuring that she couldn't hear me, I approached our back door to call out again, no response.

Being on the verge of the house step, I stepped up to open the door so I could shout one more time. To my amazement, Curly calmly followed me right up the steps. At this point, a spark of youthful prankster took over my thought processes. Would Curly follow me into the house? Let's see. I propped the door open and stepped inside. Curly followed calmly and contentedly. Amazing. Will he follow further? Sure enough! Only after I arrived in the kitchen did I shout one more time, with Curly in hand.

"Aunt Frieda, come look at my steer. I have him in the kitchen!"

"You what!" was her response, followed almost instantly by "Robert Roy! Get that animal out of this house!" from my mother as she rushed from the living room where they had been visiting. Curly meanwhile calmly stood by me, having no idea

of the human conversation erupting.

I knew I was in trouble. When my mother pulled out the "Robert Roy" instead of "Bobby," I knew I'd better take cover. So I immediately turned Curly around and headed out of the kitchen. As I exited the kitchen, both ladies followed. "Bobby, I can't believe you did that," came from Aunt Frieda. "He had better not have made a mess," from my mother.

Just as calmly as we had entered, we left the house. No harm done, just a well-earned hysterical response from two important ladies of my life. I did indeed finally get Aunt Frieda's attention. To say I had brought extra rare T-bones into the kitchen is an understatement.

Here is another student story resulting from the house plan exercise:

Unexpected Visitors
by Donna Leighton

One Sunday afternoon, my family and I were seated around the dining room table having our usual after-church dinner comprised of pot roast with cooked carrots and potatoes in our somewhat dark dining room on the lower level of the house, when suddenly the back door swung open wildly. It was located off the stairway landing, a floor above us. At first we had no idea what was happening.

Our aunt, uncle, and cousins from Wichita, Kansas, who had a history of surprising us with their visits (we lived in Illinois), yelled down the stairs while raucously laughing. "Hello, is anyone home? We're heeeere." They had an uncle on the other side of their family who lived in a different part of Illinois, and they would occasionally "pop in" to visit us after seeing him.

We all had different reactions. My seven siblings and I were thrilled to see our rambunctious and fun cousins and have them shake us out of our Sunday doldrums. We knew our day would be infinitely more interesting now. Our dad had a look on his face associated with his sister's drop-in visits akin to "here we go again." Mom was in horror at the state of the house, which in reality was always ridiculously clean and well-maintained given the size of our family, but she was mortified that people might see it in less than perfect condition. This was especially ironic because the relatives that dropped by lived in the messiest house I'd ever seen.

Suddenly, the pot roast tasted a little better and we gulped it down in order to be excused—to do the dishes of course, as quickly as possible, and then commence getting into trouble with our cousins. There were five of them, three girls and two boys and eight of us. Their family was so different than ours. They lived in the country and we lived in the city, but that was only the beginning.

Our cousins were loud and crazy and got away with behavior that would never be tolerated in our home, but their very presence got our parents to relax their usual authoritarian ways and it gave us a chance to cut loose a little more. We'd listened wide eyed as we stayed up well past our bedtime as they told stories with their Kansas twang, of purposely waving the bus onward in the mornings so they wouldn't have a way to get to school after their parents had left for work. And there was a tale of one of the brothers chasing the rest of them around the backyard with a butcher knife until the rest of them locked themselves in the chicken house. Our parents were strict disciplinarians and theirs were anything but. We couldn't imagine getting away with such behavior, but they laughed hysterically over these antics. They laughed so hard they could barely finish the story of leaving one of the kids behind at a gas station during their journey and not realizing it until about 70 miles down the road. This was unbelievable stuff to us!

The joy of seeing them was soon replaced with sadness when they left after too short a visit. There was many a Sunday the rest of the year, while sitting at the table and chewing our pot roast, that we secretly wished for our cousins to throw open the back door, yell down the stairs, and fill our lives with excitement once more.

Occasionally a student will find the exercise too difficult to do because of the bad memories it evokes. A few years ago, a student in her mid-30s began the exercise and then burst into tears. I wondered if I had said something to upset her—one of my bad jokes for instance. I talked to her and she said, "I just can't do this because I immediately am back in our very dysfunctional home where both of my parents were alcoholics and spent nearly every evening yelling and fighting." Then she said, "Would it be okay if I drew the floor plan for my tree house?" This she did. When the students began sharing their house plans, she held up the sketch of her tree house and explained that whenever her parents began fighting, she ran out of the house and climbed into her tree house, where she felt safe while watching and listening to her parents yell at each other. "These were difficult times for our family," she explained, "and this exercise brought it all back." She had tears running down her face.

The house exercise brings back both the good and bad sides of a person's memories. Some memories are so horrific that students choose not to write them, and that is their choice. Students who write about the bad memories can often become unburdened from something that may have nagged them their entire lives.

Turning Points in Life

For this exercise, I give each of my students a large piece of drawing paper (the same kind of paper used for the house plan exercise). I ask them to draw a line across the page, and indicate their birth date on the left end of the line and the current date on the other end of the line. Then along the line, they indicate the turning points in life: graduations, marriage, divorce, birth of a child, serious illness, death of a loved one, special event, etc. Then I ask them to select one or more of these turning points and write a story about it.

This is a powerful exercise, as each turning point can be highly emotional, and emotional events tend to be seared in our memories. "One of the things we know from gathering stories about people is they have powerful memories that are associated with emotion. People remember those moments. When they got married, when horrible things happened (veterans remember the horrible things from combat). People remember things so much more when there is an emotional dimension to it."[6]

As I've mentioned, I had polio when I was twelve. The emotional impact of that experience proved more devastating than the physical challenges. I have never forgotten nor have I fully gotten over the feeling of hopelessness, and even worse, a feeling of worthlessness. I was a very active farm boy and with polio I could not do all the things I was accustomed to doing. I could not play softball, my favorite game in grade school. In high school I could not play baseball or basketball—the pastimes of nearly all the boys in my high school class. I was encouraged to take a typewriting class—which, in those days, was made up entirely of girls hoping to land secretarial positions when they graduated.

After a few weeks, I discovered I enjoyed typing (manual typewriters in those days) and went on to become a reporter on the school newspaper, and eventually editor. One important reason why I am a writer today is because of my bout with polio and my inability to physically do what other boys my age were doing. Here is a story one of my writing students wrote about a turning point in his life:

Homecoming 1965
by Jim Rose

The silence was deafening. Perhaps it was the discomfort of being seated at the head of the table, which compelled me to want to say something profound. Sarah and I had been away from North Carolina for more than a year. We were pleased to come back to Pikeville to have Thanksgiving dinner with my mother's brothers and sister who lived close by. Uncle Bill and Aunt Lib were there. Aunt Annie and Uncle George, along with my Uncle John and his wife, Mickey, were there. Insisting that I sit at the head of the dining room table, my mother wanted me to take the place of my dad, who had died in October of '62. But she wasn't the only one pressuring.

On my graduation day from medical school in 1964, my Uncle Dave and Aunt Gen had sequestered Sarah and me into the tiny kitchen of our apartment in Chapel Hill, where we literally huddled together, arms around each other, in a close circle.

"I am sure," Dave said, "that once you have completed your training, you will want to come back to Pikeville to practice medicine." As a retired surgeon and a past state senator, my uncle was unaccustomed to not having his way, but I needed to make my own decisions.

It was Thanksgiving 1965, when a very popular ex-governor of North Carolina, Terry Sanford, was a candidate for the Democratic nomination for President. His opponent was the Governor of Alabama, George Wallace. As an intern in St. Louis, I had not followed the campaign, so I had no idea that school busing was an issue. In order to facilitate racial integration in the public schools, students were bussed to schools far from their homes. You could be a teacher living across the street from your school, and your own kids were legally forbidden from attending that school. Such was the situation with the family of John and Mickey. According to Mickey, policemen patrolled school hallways, one black student's throat had been

slashed in the school where she taught, and teachers were quit-
ting. George Wallace was against busing.

I said emphatically, "I do not understand why anyone would
vote for George Wallace." Never before in my life had silence
spoken to me so clearly. As a college math professor, John was
a passionate teacher. "Jimmy," he said, "you have to live here
to understand what is going on here."

That moment confirmed the importance of thinking before
speaking. Had I been more sensitive to the circumstances of my
aunts and uncles, I might have asked how they felt about the
issue of busing and whether or not it was the right thing to do.
I might have agreed with them. In either case, I suspect a more
fruitful discussion would have ensued.

Mind Mapping

I introduce all of my writing students to mind mapping, a rather easy way
to wake up one's memory. Mind mapping, different from merely listing
ideas or thoughts that come to mind, is a way to trigger memories, but also
a way to show relationships of memories to each other. Some people refer
to mind mapping as clustering. Rico writes, "Just as many natural forms
come in clusters—grapes, lilacs, spider eggs, cherries—so thoughts and
images, when given free rein seem to come in clusters of associations…
Clustering is a nonlinear brainstorming process akin to free association."[7]
Here's what I tell students to do:

1. Draw a circle in the middle of a large blank sheet of paper.
   Write the idea you want to focus on in that circle. In my
   workshops I often assign the topic, "What was your first job for
   pay?" and ask workshop participants to mind map that topic.
   If you want to unearth memories about your mother, write,
   "Mom" in the center circle, and so on.

2. Focus on the center circle. As you recall something, quickly
   draw a line from the center circle, make another circle at the
   end of the line, and write this recollection in it. Don't stop to
   dwell on what you have written but rapidly continue to draw
   circles. As you think of ideas related to the most recent circle,
   write them and draw further circles around them. Soon you will
   have many circles around the larger circle in the center. This
   process is one way to tap into the creative part of the brain—the

right brain as some psychologists have called it. The reason to hurry, making circle after circle, is to avoid having the judging side of your brain say things such as, "This doesn't look like it's going anywhere," or "Why are you doing this foolishness when you should be working on your story?"

3. Keep in mind that there is no right or wrong way to mind map—these are your memories that are surfacing and this is one way to not only recognize them as they bubble out of the recesses of your mind, but it also shows the relationship of these ideas to each other.

I've discovered something else, which is one of the strengths of mind mapping. As thoughts emerge, they trigger other thoughts and yet more thoughts after that. I've had writing students tell me that after a session of mind mapping—I usually give my students about fifteen minutes to do it in the workshops—they recalled things that they have long thought were forgotten.

Of course when you are alone, you can take as long as you wish to mind map topics. I remember once when I was flying from Chicago to Denver, I mind mapped a topic the entire way, which ended up being about two and a half hours.

When students finish with the mind mapping exercise, I ask them to look at the page of circles and write a story that relates to one or several of them. Some of the stories are brief, really introductions to longer stories. Here is an example:

First Job For Pay
by Kathy Macleod

They put me on bread and butter. It was my first week working on the food line in our hospital cafeteria, preparing patient trays. It was easy work, and I was marveling that I was actually being paid $1.60 an hour to place two pieces of white bread and two pats of butter on trays. I idly gazed up the line and, seeing the two slightly older girls in meat and vegetables, the hot section that required portioning, I wondered if I might ever be as important as them.

Here is another story one of my writing students recalled after doing the map mapping exercise. The author was a retired juvenile probation officer in Iowa.

Saved
by Bob Galloway

*He was no longer than the minute hand of a clock and just as
thin. He was cheerful. A wide smile flicked across his freckled
face. His sandy hair darted in all directions. He wore a new
long-sleeved blue work shirt. His new blue bib overalls were
a size too large. He wore new high-topped work shoes. As he
squirmed in the high backed chair, he swung his feet above the
pine board floor.*

*On the high bench, the iron-gray-headed Irish judge, with forty
years of judicial experience, was perched in his overstuffed
leather chair like some barn owl waiting for his prey. The
judge, in his deep gravelly voice, recited the litany of charges.
The list detailed how the twelve-year-old boy and his ten-year-
old sister had broken into a trailer home, stealing some soda
pop and some small change. Upon leaving the trailer, they had
turned on all the water faucets, causing considerable water
damage to the trailer. They had stolen a corn picker and driven
it through the side of a barn. At the Keokuk Yacht club, they cut
ten pleasure boats loose from their moorings, allowing them
to drift down the Mississippi River before crashing into lock
19, and they broke out windows at the elementary school. The
judge ended by stating that this was the boy's third appearance
in court in less than a year. The newly hired probation officer
was startled.*

"Do you like to come here to see me?" the judge inquired.

"No sir."

*"I notice you have on new clothes and new shoes on each
occasion."*

*"Yes, sir. Ma and Pa want me to look my best. I even took a tub
bath."*

*The judge coughed to hide his smile. The parents stared blankly
at the ceiling. The mother was petite but had large rough
hands. She was homely and looked twice her thirty years. The
father looked taller than he was because he seemed to be all
long arms and legs. His face also looked long, maybe due to his*

long pointed nose and pointed chin. He was tanned and leathery looking. He was a sixty-year-old unemployed laborer who liked to brag that he bought his wife for $1.00 from her father, a migrant farm boss. The father didn't want her because she was "retarded."

When the young probation officer had arrived at the boy's home for his first interview, the mother greeted him by saying she had to go milk the cow. She stood in the doorway barefooted with the buttons down the front of her dress undone. She was not wearing underwear and was no Marilyn Monroe!

"Where's your husband?" inquired the officer.

"He's drunk."

According to the official report, the family home sat alone along the Des Moines River. It was a shack built from discarded tin, cracked glass, old warped boards, and slats. It had a dirt floor. The old man worked on his housing project in sober moments and some not so sober moments. The place looked like something out of Al Capp's Dogpatch. Dogs, cats, pigs, and an old sow wandered in and out to find food on the kitchen floor. Mice darted out from their hiding places. The living room was sparsely furnished. A console black and white television was stationed in a corner in front of a battered couch. The kids liked watching TV. So did the chickens that were sitting on the arms and backs of the couch. They helped color the couch with white streaks.

The judge grunted as he read the probation officer's report. He shifted uncomfortably in his chair and stared out the window. He hated juvenile cases. He never knew what to do. This family wasn't civilized. Iowans were supposed to be educated and civilized. He looked up at the boy and his court appointed attorney. "No budding Clarence Darrow," thought the judge.

"What do you do when you skip school?" asked the judge.

"I fish, sir. I hunt frogs and snakes. I toss stones in the river. When I'm bored I find other things to do."

The judge arched his eyebrows. "Like breaking into trailers and stealing corn pickers?"

"Sir, I don't mean no harm to anyone. I'm just fooling around."

The judge had started to say something when the father jumped up. "Your highness, we was planning to go to Arkansas to live with relatives until me and the Mrs. find work."

The judge suddenly seemed happy. "Probation Officer Gallo-way, please arrange an interstate compact agreement for the boy's supervision. Oh yes, and make sure the family leaves the county safely. Soon! Case closed."

"God help the state of Arkansas," mumbled the judge as he skipped back to his office.

In the early stages of writing a story, I draw circle after circle. Other writers make lists, jot down memories as fast as they can without judging which are important and which not. With both mind mapping and list making, you are doing personal brainstorming, with one memory triggering another. It is important to jot down your memories. Even though you have the tidbit of a memory—something you haven't thought about for years—such tidbits have the uncanny ability of disappearing. When working on a story, you'll discover that snippets of memory will arrive when you least expect them. Just before you go to sleep. When you wake up in the middle of the night. When you are driving. When you are doing something physical. For me, working in my garden or chopping wood or hiking on my farm often results in new memories. Thoughts seem to come out of the blue. To make sure I capture them, I carry a pen and some 3 x 5" notecards. I have some cards by my bedside as well, so whenever a memory arrives I jot it down.

More Memory Triggers

Many of my students have also found these activities useful in bringing back memories, especially the older people in my classes.

- **Visit museums and historic sites with exhibits representing the years you are writing about.**
- **Listen to music of the time.**
- **Look at old photos.**
- **Sit down with siblings, relatives, or old friends and swap stories of the time you are interested in.**

- **Review old Sears Roebuck or Montgomery Ward catalogs.**

Many historical societies have collections of these old catalogs. Select a catalog for the year when you were twelve. There you will find the clothing, toys, kitchen implements, furniture— about everything that was common in homes during that time. What you see will trigger memories of items that you grew up with, and further, as you write your stories, you can check your memory for accuracy.

- **Look at old newspapers (available at historical societies).**

I especially appreciate the ads in the newspapers of the years when I was growing up. I am reminded of what was available in the grocery stores and what the items cost. The clothing of the day. The kinds of automobiles available. Merely thumbing through an old newspaper, reading the ads, but also reading the news articles can bring back many memories. If you are of my generation, what were you doing on December 7, 1941, when the Japanese bombed Pearl Harbor? When the war ended in 1945? When the student protests were going on during the 1960s, and so on.

- **Visit antique stores.**

For me, and for others of my generation, visiting an antique store is like going home. When I see a kerosene lamp, I am immediately back in our farm house where a kerosene lamp had a prominent place on the kitchen table. Seeing the antique kerosene lamp reminds me of doing school work by the feeble yellow light, eating our meals, playing cards, and everything else we did on long cold winter nights when it was dark by 4:30 and wasn't daylight much before 7:30 the following morning.

Recently I bought an old blacksmith-made cowbell in an antique store. It still had the leather strap that went around the cow's neck. The cowbell, with its clear, "dong, dong," took me back to the summer nights when we sat on the back porch of our farm house when the chores were done and listened to the sounds of a summer night, a whippoorwill calling its name in the distance, and the sound of the cow bell telling us that the neighbor's cows were grazing in their night pasture and all was well.

When I see an old three-tined pitchfork, my mind immediately returns to the years when I had a close relationship with such a fork. In fact I had my own pitchfork, as did my brothers and my dad. I recall working on a threshing crew and pitching oat bundles into a threshing machine. I remember the long hot days in late June and July when we "made hay," pitching the cured alfalfa and clover onto a steel-wheeled wagon pulled by a team of horses. At the farm I own now, my shed is filled with old tools, each one evoking a memory and each with a story.

- **Visit the place where you grew up.**

A couple years ago, I worked with public television on an hour-long documentary titled "A Farm Story with Jerry Apps." For one part of the documentary, we returned to my home farm, where they filmed me walking up the driveway to the farmhouse where I was born and raised. It was a powerful moment, for as I walked up the driveway that winter day, the memories of my childhood came rushing back. I remembered the many days when my brothers and I walked down that driveway to the dusty country road that trailed by our farm. We were on our way to the one-room country school, which was a mile away. I walked into the now unused barn where we housed our small herd of dairy cows. And although no cows have been in the barn, the smells and the memories lingered. Cold mornings milking cows by hand in the light of a kerosene lantern. Hot summer days when we hauled hay into the upper reaches of the barn. The frightful day when a windstorm nearly toppled the structure, killing calves and injuring cows. The memories both pleasant and not so pleasant came rushing back, as did the stories.

Visiting the old neighborhood and the apartment or house where you grew up can often provide a wonderful trigger for memories as well as provide valuable details—what the landscape looks like, for instance. Revisit the hills and valleys, the lakes and streams, schools and churches—become reacquainted with the surroundings of your youth. Although the landscape may have changed considerably since you left the area, assuming that you left, there remains enough of the landscape of your youth to both trigger memories as well as provide background details for your story. You may want to visit where you lived when first married, where you served in the military, and so on.

- **Review family records.**

My mother was the record keeper in our family. She noted every nickel of income on our small family farm, as well as every dime of expense and often joked, as did my father, that for many years, expenses on the farm seemed to exceed income.

Both my mother and father died in 1993, and as the oldest son—I have two brothers—my wife and I had the task of cleaning out their home and making it ready for sale. In one of the bureau drawers, we found the farm records that she started keeping in 1926, when she and my dad moved onto the farm, until 1973, when they sold the farm and moved to town. As I paged through these record books, all neatly written in pencil, the memories began flooding back. I was born in 1934, so starting about 1936 and the years that followed until I left home in 1951, I remembered the events connected with the entries. It only took reading a particular entry for me to remember a story connected with it. For instance, one of the entries written in 1946 was "Hoe – $1.15." Pa had purchased a new garden hoe from Hotz's Hardware in Wild Rose. Upon reading that simple expense entry, I remembered stories of hoeing the garden, hoeing our potato patch, hoeing the strawberry patch, hoeing out the quack grass that grew in the hollows in the cornfield—hoeing whenever there wasn't something more important to do on the farm. Here is what I wrote:

When you are twelve years old, to survive hoeing, you either had to make your mind go blank or imagine exotic things. You also had to keep an eye on Pa as you moved down a row, chopping out weeds. If you slipped and chopped off a potato plant, he wouldn't say anything. But do it a second time and you were in trouble.

A two-acre potato patch didn't look like much compared to a twenty-acre hayfield. But when you were hoeing, two acres was immense. The sun baked your hide, sweat ran down your back and collected around your middle, and more sweat streamed down your forehead and pooled in your eyes. You tried to ignore these discomforts as you worked on those mind-clearing or exotic thoughts. Just when you had it down—the clear mind, for instance—Pa piped up with a question.

"You know the difference between pigweed and ragweed?"

"Huh?"

"You goin' deaf? What's the difference 'tween a pigweed and ragweed?"

I wanted to say I didn't much care about telling one weed from another. I thought I was doing good when I could tell potato plants from weeds.

"No, I don't," I answered. So much for a clear mind. Now I sensed the hot sun on my back and the rivers of sweat running over me, and I had to think besides.

Pa launched into a detailed discussion of pigweed and ragweed. He told me what they looked like when they were small, what they looked like when they were bigger, and how tall they grew if you missed one with your hoe.

As long as Pa was so talkative, I decided to ask him about something else—something in the exotic-thinking category. I tried to figure out how to introduce the topic as I kept the hoe moving.

"I've been wondering about bulls and cows," I finally said.

"What about bulls and cows?"

I hesitated, took off my straw hat, and swiped a red handkerchief across my sweaty head, then ran the handkerchief around the inside of my hat—something I'd seen Pa do often.

"I was wondering how they know to get together—how they know to breed?"

A slow smile spread over Pa's face. "Oh, they just do. It's natural."

I kept on hoeing and thinking about Pa's answer and wondering if that's how it worked with people.

Several minutes passed as we hoed in silence and I thought my exotic thoughts. I glanced up at the sun to figure out the time—we had at least another hour before noon. Instantly, my mind filled with pictures of mashed potatoes, canned beef, fresh lettuce, and strawberries. It's surprising how fast hunger replaces everything else a twelve-year old boy has on his mind when he's hoeing.[8]

- **Recall sayings.**

  My dad had a head full of one-liners. When I remember the line, I also remember the stories associated with it. One of his favorites: when someone began talking about kids getting into trouble, he would say, "A tired kid is a good kid." By that he meant, keeping your kids busy doing chores not only helps get the necessary work done, but it tires the kids. I speak from experience, as on the home farm there were never-ending chores to be done, from the time we got up in the morning until we went to bed at night. Of course we got a break from doing chores when school was in session, with chores before and after school.

  Another saying my father often used with me and my brothers, and with himself as he grew older and couldn't do the things he did when he was young: "Do the best you can with what you've got." He applied that bit of advice in many settings—often leading to stories. For example, he never was one to say that he expected my brothers and me to earn straight A's in school, to excel in sports, or to do public speaking. He merely wanted us to make sure that we were doing the best we could possibly do—not always trying to compare ourselves with others, but always comparing ourselves with ourselves.

  I will never forget when he was in his nineties and still working in his garden and I asked him how he was doing. I knew what the answer would be, and I heard it once more. "I'm doing the best I can with what I've got." He died six weeks after that conversation.

  Although my father always supported and encouraged my brothers and me to get as much education as possible, he also often reminded us with these words, "Just because you have a lot of education doesn't mean you know anything." This likely came from the fact that he had been pulled out of school after completing fifth grade to go to work, a not too uncommon practice for farm people of his generation. What he meant, of course, was common sense and practical knowledge was equally and often more important than "book learning."

  One way to write about people you know is to capture their sayings, and many people have them. It is a way of getting at the core of their beliefs, and besides, those reading your stories will generally find these sayings interesting. When my father died in 1993, I wrote across the top of a page in my journal, "Things

I learned from my father." I thought I would complete this assignment, one way of grieving his passing, in a few days. It was a couple of weeks later that I found myself still writing down these "Learnings," many of which were sayings. I gathered what I had written in my journal, expanded on some of it, and included all of this in a book titled *Rural Wit and Wisdom* (Fulcrum Publishing, 2012). The book has gone through several reprints and revisions and has sold thousands of copies and is still in print. A picture of my father is on the cover.

5

Research and How to Do It

When my writing students ask me how I spend my writing time, I tell them I spend one-third of my time researching, one-third writing, one-third re-writing, and one-third doing promotion and marketing. I also remind them that I was never very good at math. I spend many hours researching—digging out background information, checking facts against my memory, filling in the blank spaces in my memory, and much more.

I've always enjoyed doing research. I am forever turning up ideas, perspectives, and bits of history that prove important for my stories. Researching takes time and occasionally is more than a little challenging. So why do it? Why not rely on your memory to create your stories and let it go at that? You can do that, of course, and it's not uncommon for some storytellers to follow this approach. But for me, especially because I believe that all of our stories, no matter how we eventually share them, should first be written, I want my facts and figures to be as accurate as possible. For example, when I wrote a story about the end of World War II and my memories about that (see chapter 3), I remembered it was the summer of 1945, but I did not remember the exact date. I checked and found out it was August 14, 1945.

Research also adds details and descriptions to our stories. When I describe people in my stories, if I don't have a photograph to tell me what kind of clothing he or she wore, I go to old newspapers and old catalogs to see how people dressed.

I once wanted to write a story about the hired man on our farm in 1944, Henry Lackelt, who taught me to drive in his 1925 Model T Ford Touring car. I remembered the event well: how Henry had me practice in the cow pasture just south of the barn, and how proud I was that he let me drive his Model T.

But I couldn't remember exactly what the car looked like, so I researched the model so I could tell the story accurately. The Model T had no shifting lever, but rather had three pedals on the floor, one for forward, one for reverse, and one for the brake. You hand-cranked it to get it started, and you controlled the speed of the engine with a lever on the steering wheel. The car had a cloth top that you could put up and down—today we'd call it a convertible. The results of my research helped me paint a picture of the car in the reader's mind and also helped me remember how it felt to drive it.

I also research the background or context for my stories. When I wrote about what conditions were like on the home farm during the Depression, I jotted down my memories of our farm and our neighborhood during those years. But I didn't remember or perhaps didn't know how the Depression affected those living in other parts of the country, especially urban areas. But a few hours of research gave me the background information I needed for the stories I wrote. See *Letters from Hillside Farm* (Fulcrum Press, 2013) as an example.

For my research, I also do extensive interviewing (below I describe the interview methods that I use). For instance, when my parents were in their late 80s, I spent several hours interviewing them (I recorded all the interviews). Not only did I obtain stories I had not heard before, but I also had on tape the way that they spoke. How they used words, and formed sentences. This was important because when I wrote stories about them, I wanted to accurately portray their words and how they used them.

Is it necessary to complete the research before beginning to write a story? Here's what I do. I do a certain amount research before I start writing a story; how much depends on how rich my memory is on the topic. But almost always, during the process of writing, I discover I must do additional research. The process of creating a story becomes a dynamic one. I start with my memory, I do some background research, and I begin writing. I usually discover that I need more information, so I do more research, continue writing, continue researching, and so on. Because I write against contract deadlines, I must complete a writing project by a given date. Without deadlines, some of my stories and the writing and research would go on indefinitely. Some beginning story writers who do not have contract deadline may find it useful to establish a deadline—even though it can be tentative and adjusted as the work progresses.

When researching my stories, I look within two broad categories:

1. Primary or original research sources and
2. Secondary research sources.

Primary Research Sources

Primary sources are original, first-hand accounts or reports of events.

Your Memory

Your memory is an important, if not the most important, primary research source for writing your personal stories. But sometimes it needs a little help to fill in the blanks and correct errors.

Public Records

Property records, court records, police records, military records, census reports, and cemetery records are excellent primary research sources. Many of these records are online these days. Other places to find them are in newspaper archives and county courthouses. The National Archives in Washington, DC is an excellent source of military records. I also have found local and state historical societies a rich source of primary research materials. I am often able to find old newspapers printed during the era I am writing about, including the ads that tell me much about the material culture of the day—what people wore, the kinds of automobiles they drove, and so on. By reading the ads in these old newspapers, I am able to determine the prices of such things as a pound of hamburger or a loaf of bread during the time in which my story is set.

When I wrote the story of my farm (*Old Farm: A History,* Wisconsin Historical Society Press, 2008), I wanted to learn more about the man who homesteaded the place. I went to the Wisconsin Historical Society website, where there are lists of Civil War veterans from Wisconsin. Once I found Tom Stewart's name and his unit, I contacted the National Archives in Washington, DC. From the archives, I received a wealth of valuable information about Mr. Stewart, including when he was married, the names of his children, and the nature of his injury during the war.

Private Records

Photographs, journals, scrapbooks, letters. These are rich sources of primary research material, which I use often. Remember that these are private records, and you will need permission from the holder to use the material in your stories. (It's not a bad idea to get that permission in writing.) Also remember that some of the material you uncover may be controversial or show a person in a negative light.

Serendipity

Almost always in my research, I find something that I wasn't looking for. It may be a casual comment from someone I interview. It may be the book next to the one on the library shelf that I am looking for. It may be a document attached to a letter I've found. These unintended research findings can make all the difference for the story I'm writing.

For example, when I was researching the story of the Ringling Brother's Circus, (*Ringlingville USA*, Wisconsin Historical Society Press, 2005), I learned from one of my interviewees that there might be another major source of Ringling records beyond the ones I already knew about. This interviewee told me that he remembered hearing that a circus fan in Columbus, Ohio had purchased some Ringling records at an antique auction. He knew the person and gave me his name and telephone number. I contacted this man, and soon I was in the basement of his home poring over the original account books for the circus, written in longhand by Otto Ringling, who was one of the five Ringling Brothers. This proved to be extremely important information, allowing me to share financial information about the Ringling Bros. Circus that had not been previously published.

While researching, I try to keep my eyes and ears open to sources that I may not have known about, and I don't hesitate in following up on the leads. In many ways, being a researcher is like being a detective, as I look for clues and follow up on leads in order to find the answers to my questions. Information that you weren't looking for but uncover can lead to questions you hadn't even thought about, and storylines that prove both interesting and provocative.

Interviews

Interviews with family members and other people can also be important primary research sources. I gained much valuable information that I have incorporated into many of my stories from relatives, especially my parents. If you are writing about your growing up years, important people to interview are those who knew you as a child. I've found a most reliable source to be your aunts—if you want the truth about what you were like as a child. They know what you were like, and they are not reluctant to share their thoughts either. While your mother may have thought and likely told you that you were a near perfect child, the aunts reveal the truth.

Tools for Interviewing

I use a relatively inexpensive digital recorder, the kind that, once I have recorded an interview, I can plug into a USB port on my computer to save the files. My recorder has a simple phone adapter that I can use for phone interviews.

Before the Interview

I always begin by writing down the questions I want to ask. And although I'll have my notes with me during the interview, I memorize them in advance. Nothing stifles an interview more than mechanically going through your questions: "The first question I want to ask you…" and so on. Try to make the interview a conversation between two people. Also, make sure that your questions require more than a yes or no answer. For example, if you are interviewing one of your aunts and ask, "Do you remember what I was like as a child?" the aunt could answer, "Yes, I do," and say no more. A better question would be, "Tell me what I was like when I was a child, as you remember."

As a practical matter, before each interview I put fresh batteries in my recorder, and practice to make sure I remember how to use it. Some years ago I was interviewing a college official in North Carolina, and in the middle of the interview the batteries went dead. Ever since that day—it had taken me weeks to gain this person's permission for an interview—I put fresh batteries in my recorder before every interview.

Before the interview, I ask the person's permission to record the session. Most people agree, but occasionally someone will say no. I gently remind the person I am recording to make sure I have an accurate record of what they are telling me, and that I don't want to quote them incorrectly in my story. This statement almost always works. After more than forty years of interviewing people, I have had but one or two people who absolutely refused to be recorded. For these people, I took notes as rapidly as I could, hoping I was able to catch the essence of what they said.

Let your interview subject know in advance what you plan to talk about, to give her some time to think about her responses. And tell her approximately how long the interview will take. It can be hard to predict this, but people like to know what kind of time commitment they're making. With older interviewees, you might want to plan for shorter interviews. You can always continue the conversation another day. When I interviewed my father when he was in his late eighties, I kept the interviews no longer than forty-five minutes or so, and I did several interviews with him over a period of weeks. Each interview focused on a single topic.

If the person I want to interview lives some distance away or is too busy to meet with me face to face, I do the interview over the phone. My digital recorder has a simple device that easily picks up both my and the interviewee's voice. Again, be sure the person understands that you are recording the conversation.

Finally, before we get started I make some small talk—a little "warmup" for both me and my interviewee. I tell the person a little about the story I am writing and perhaps share my personal history if it seems relevant. Mik Derks, a longtime public television producer who has conducted hundreds of interviews, told me, "I need to establish trust with the person interviewed. It's important that I show interest in what the person is saying. This gives the interviewee the feeling that what they are saying is important and gives them permission to remember and share more of their story. I try to get people comfortable enough in the interview so they will share their feelings."[9]

Next I turn on the recorder (and check to make sure it is recording), mention the date and time, and ask the person to say his or her name and spell it if it's difficult.

During the Interview

Remember to listen. The person might need time to think between questions, and there will be pauses. Don't feel compelled to talk at those times. When your interviewee remembers a story, allow her to continue, even if the story seems a bit distant from the question you asked. Without a doubt, her stories will add interest and depth to the interview.

Often, after hearing a response to one of your questions, you will want to probe more deeply. "Can you remember any more about that? What's an example of what you are talking about? Do you remember a story about that situation?" A general guide to asking questions includes answers to "Who, what, where, when, why, and how?" Occasionally the person you are interviewing will turn the tables on you and begin interviewing you. Remain polite but keep control of the interview.

After the Interview

For face-to-face interviews, when I am back in my car, or at home if I have not traveled far for the interview, I immediately write down something about the background setting for the interview. I also note some of the physical characteristics of the person I interviewed. Later, when writing a story, I often include some of this descriptive information. In addition, writing notes describing the person and the setting helps me remember the discussion more clearly, especially if my list of interviewees is long.

As soon as possible after the interview, I plug my recorder into my computer, listen to it and begin transcribing the interview so I will have a hard copy. As I transcribe, I do some editing, taking out the "ahs" and "you knows" and the redundancy that is natural in most interviews. If I discover during the transcription process that I want further information, or there is something said that I don't understand, I contact the person.

I save all of my interview recordings. If a reader tells me he didn't say something I've attributed to him, I can dig out my recording. I might be overly cautious; in all my years of interviewing people, no one has told me I misquoted him.

When Family Members Don't Agree

It is not unusual when interviewing family members to discover they don't agree with each other, and their memory of the event may also differ from yours. My twin brothers are three and one-half years younger than I am. Events that I remember well, they remember little or not at all. For instance I remember when our Grandfather Witt died in 1941. I was seven years old at the time, they were three. They did not remember his passing.

Occasionally, my brothers remember something quite differently than I do. For instance in one of my books I wrote about memories of a Thanksgiving dinner held at our Aunt Louise's farm. The three us agreed that Uncle Roy had big ears. Who could forget those big ears? But we differed in our memories of their dog. I remembered the dog's name was Ralph. Brother Donald agreed. Brother Darrel insisted it was something else. At moments like this, two out of three was good enough for me to go with Ralph as the dog's name.

Also, when I discuss this point with my writing students, I remind them that they are entitled to their own memories, and that it's unlikely that people will remember an event in exactly the same way. That is not to deny the importance of doing research to check on facts—such as the ending day for World War II, and a description of a Model T Ford car, that I mentioned earlier. But when telling personal stories, *personal* is the key word.

Secondary Research Sources

Secondary sources are accounts written after an event by someone who was not an eyewitness. They sometimes include valuable analysis and perspectives that come only with the passage of time. They can be found in books of all sorts, including biographies, encyclopedias, dictionaries, textbooks, almanacs, atlases, and the Internet.

The Internet

The Internet is a rich source of information, but a source that must be used with caution. Using the Internet requires a bit of skill in determining what is accurate and what may be inaccurate information. When I begin a project, say I am writing about my memories growing up during the Depression, I check the Internet to find who has researched and written about the Depressions years. There are thousands of entries. I then look for the information source—was it done by a reputable researcher, who may be a university professor or associated with a historical society or another reputable source? I try to determine if what I am reading is fact or opinion—these two perspectives are sometimes tangled on the Internet.

If I want to learn about the history of a town, say the town where my grandfather grew up, I can type in the town's name. Most towns, cities, and counties have websites, and they can usually be trusted to post accurate information. Almost all government agencies have websites that provide valuable details and background information for your stories.

Libraries

I regularly use public libraries, university research libraries, and historical society libraries as major research sources for my storytelling work. Often the reference librarian will help me find the books and other reference materials that will help me develop the context for the story I'm writing. Libraries also have websites, which can be useful sources of information.

Keeping Research Records

Occasionally I meet a person who does excellent research but doesn't take the time to record it. Ultimately this person doesn't know what she has or how to find it. Record keeping is essential and there are many ways of doing it.

I've created a simple inventory system for all my research findings. What I do is generate a paper copy of each piece of research, whether it is a transcript from an interview, notes I've made reading a book, facts I've gotten from an encyclopedia, or articles I've gotten off the Internet. I number each piece of research and place the material in either three-ring binders or in folders for a file box if the project is a large one. I create a computer file for each item, with the title and brief description of the item. When I want to find a particular piece of research, I type in key words, which leads me to the number of the item. I then go to my files and find the item.

There are other ways to organize research material. What's important is that you have some kind of system so you can retrieve a piece of research when you want it. For me, there are few things more frustrating than knowing I have a particular piece of information and I can't find it.

Striving for Accuracy

As I have mentioned, we are each entitled to our own memories, especially the meaning and emotion that we attach to events and people that we remember, and the effect they have had on our lives. These are ours to share or not share. But our memories can play tricks on us concerning details—and here is where research can help.

Sometimes, as we attempt to provide background details for our stories, we include something that is an error. Let's say we are including information about a distant relative who farmed in the early 1860s, and we want to provide some detail to make the story more interesting. We write that Joseph kept his cattle confined in a pasture surrounded by barbwire fence. That would be impossible, as barbwire was not invented until 1873. And if you believe no one will catch the error, someone will.

6

Journaling

I started keeping a journal when I was twelve years old. That's not to say that I have written in it every day since then, because I have not. But these many years later, I do write something in my journal once or twice a week. I record the weather; I note recent activities, the good and the bad, the joys and the disappointments, and my reactions and feeling toward what I have experienced. Sometimes as I write, a great load lifts from my shoulders. It's almost as if my troubles are transferred to my journal, when it's my troubles I choose to write about. My journals provide me with a rich source of both facts and stories about my life; I draw on them regularly for my writing.

Benefits from Journaling

Clarifies Thoughts, Feelings, and Observations

When I don't understand something, and this happens often, I begin writing about this thing, this idea, or this person. As I write, what has been troubling me becomes more clear.

When I face a problem that I don't quite understand or I can't figure out a way to solve it, I write about it in my journal. The process of writing about the problem sometimes, not always, leads to a solution.

A Path to the Subconscious

As I write, I often uncover thoughts and ideas I didn't know I had. I've seen it happen to other people as well. An older woman attending one of my writing classes informed the writing class and me, when I talked about journaling and the benefits from doing it, "I have never written in a journal and don't intend to start now." She said it as if she really meant it.

As a long-time teacher of adults, I've learned to never argue with an 80-year-old woman. So I merely said, "That's your choice, of course." And we moved on with the discussion.

The morning after Mabel (not her real name) made her announcement in the workshop, I met her on the way to the dining hall and asked her how she had slept.

"Not well at all," she said.

Before I had an opportunity to ask why, she proceeded to say, without a hint of a smile, "And it was your fault."

I mumbled something along the lines of "What did I do?", but I don't know if she even heard me before she said, "You know that dumb discussion we had about journaling in class yesterday?"

"Yes," I muttered.

"Well, I woke up at three o'clock this morning, took out some paper, and began writing. And I've been writing steadily right up to now, when it's time for breakfast."

Gathering up the gumption to inquire further, I asked, "And what did you write about?"

Her answer about knocked my socks off, because what she said was, "I don't know. My pen was moving so fast I don't know what was showing up on paper. I can't wait to get back to my room to see what I had to say."

She had experienced what other journal writers, me included, have experienced. Writing in a journal is one way of tapping into a person's unconscious, uncovering memories that the person may not have thought about for years. That was clearly the case with Mable, who not only surprised me with what she had experienced, but clearly surprised herself.

A Historical Record

My journal provides a historical record for me. Some of my writing students tell me that they have good memories and they can remember the important events in their lives, but I challenge them by saying, "You may remember the important events, but it is unlikely you remember all the details. And it is the details that give depth and provide interest in your stories."

This is certainly the case for me. For example, a few years ago I wrote a book called *Garden Wisdom: Lessons Learned from Sixty Years of Gardening* (Wisconsin Historical Society Press, 2012). I remembered much of what my gardening experiences were like over the years, but I couldn't remember exactly when and what we faced when we moved our garden from a location several hundred yards from the cabin to one only fifty yards away. I found the answer in my 1984 journal.

Sunday, October 14, 1984
Roshara, Wild Rose, Wisconsin

Ruth and I are at the farm this weekend; we arrived yesterday. Dad drove out from Wild Rose and we attached the plow to my Farmall A tractor, no small task. We intended to plow the field in front of the cabin and turn it into a garden. The field had not been plowed for more than ten years and box elder trees had popped up everywhere. We sawed them off and pulled the stumps from the ground with the tractor. We also removed a huge clump of wild berry bushes, which I cut with a scythe.

With the field cleared of trees, brambles, and brush, I plowed it so that next spring we can plant our garden here—and have access to water if necessary. One of the shortcomings of our old garden spot is we depended entirely on the rain. Now during a dry spell, we can do a little watering.

In my journal, I record important happenings in my family, both the sad and the joyful. This information, too, becomes an important historical document. Here are entries I wrote when my wife's mother died. They help me remember the details of those sad days just after her death.

Monday, December 3, 1984

Ruth's mother died at 5:30 this morning at age 87 (Ella Olson). She suffered a second massive stroke last Thursday evening and has been unconscious since. I'm surely glad she had a chance to spend a couple weeks with us here in Madison last October when she was feeling good and still involved with several craft projects that she always worked on. The funeral will be either next Wednesday or Thursday. Ruth's dad died last year, shortly after Labor Day.

Wednesday, December 5, 1984

Twelve degrees this morning. No snow, but frosty. Tomorrow is Ruth's mother's funeral.

Sunday, December 9, 1984

Warm. Mid-40s. The little snow that fell last Wednesday night that made the streets slippery has all disappeared. Last Thursday was Ruth's mother's funeral. A sad day. Ruth was very close to her mother and she is having a tough time with her loss. The funeral was nice—very similar to her dad's, which was only a year ago. It was held in the little country church just down the valley from their farm, the church the Olson family had attended for many years.

In recent years Ruth talked on the phone with her mother every Sunday evening. And she also made many trips to Viroqua, where her mother lived in an apartment. Tonight Ruth said, "I guess I won't need to drive over to Viroqua anymore."

Too bad this had to happen so close to Christmas. It will be a tough holiday season for Ruth. Our kids will all be home and that will help.

Deciding What Is Important

Writing in my journal forces me to consider what is important in my life. I don't have time to record everything that is happening—none of us do. But what I choose to write turns out to be what is most important at the time, by the very reason that I am writing about it.

A Place to Vent Frustrations

I spent several years as an administrator at the University of Wisconsin–Madison. Invariably, someone would do something that would irritate me and make me so angry I wanted to confront the person and tell them what I thought of them. But I didn't. Rather, that evening I wrote a blistering letter to this person, venting my anger and frustration with this person in language that ought never be seen in print. Of course I wrote the letter in my journal, knowing full well that it would never be mailed and the person would never see what I had said. The next morning, I felt better. My emotions had calmed down and I sat with the person and in a reasoned way (I hope) tried to explain to the person what I considered he had done wrong.

A Scrapbook

One of my long-time colleagues at the University of Wisconsin recently died and I put his obituary in my journal. When we attended a live Garrison Keillor show, I taped a ticket in my journal. So not only is my journal a series of my writings, it is also a scrapbook-like collection of people and events that have been important in my life. When I want to write about any of these things later, in one of my stories, I can turn to my journal for the detail that I need.

Journaling and Stories

I don't usually write a complete story in my journal. In fact, when I record whatever it is I'm writing on a particular day, I usually don't have a specific story in mind. But looking back at a journal entry later will often trigger a story idea.

For example, I have kept a detailed journal of my many canoe trips to the Boundary Waters Canoe Wilderness Area in northern Minnesota. In 1986, my youngest son, Jeff, and I decided to canoe in a segment of the canoe area that we hadn't visited before. Unfortunately, we canoed into the area with only a simple map that a forest ranger sketched on the back of an envelope (not a good idea). This is what I wrote in my journal:

August 20, 1986, 8:35 pm, Lake Polly

The days are much shorter now—it is nearly dark as I am writing. A loon has been circling in front of our campsite, making its distinctive call. How I love that mystical call, knowing that generations of people have enjoyed and tried to understand its mysterious nature.

A rainstorm rumbled through last night with a display of noise and light—and the pounding of rain drops on the tent roof. What a great sound for sleeping. The rain continued past noon and then stopped. A stiff northwest wind came up and the waves made for challenging canoeing.

About 2:00 p.m. we canoed to Lake Koma to try fishing there, but no luck. The Lake Koma trip involved three portages, two around river rapids and one long, one-hundred-rod portage. Our biggest problem on this trip is not having a decent map. We had great difficulty finding the portages. We searched for forty-five minutes to find the north portage to Lake Polly. We did come upon several young women sunbathing in the nude, much to their and our surprise.

What I have written is a report of a day's activities while canoing in the BWCA, but it is not a story. However, there are details in the entry that may lead to a story. In 2011, I wrote a book about my adventures in the BWCA (*Campfires and Loon Calls*, Fulcrum Publishing, 2011). While I was working on the book, I drew heavily on my journal entries, as well as on my memory. When I came across this 1986 entry, and read the line about young women sunbathing in the nude, my memory kicked in and I wrote the following story of our adventure that day.

On that late August day in 1986, the rain continued through breakfast as we sat under our rain fly, savoring second cups of coffee and gazing out at the rain enshrouded Lake Polly. My son, Jeff, and I were canoing in the Boundary Waters Canoe Wilderness Area in Northern Minnesota. In late morning, a breeze came up from the west, the sun burned through the clouds, and our dreary spirits soared.

"Good fishing day," I said.

"But how about a better lake, maybe one with fish in it," said Jeff.

I had scratched Lake Koma on my hurriedly made map, but had not indicated the location of the portage from Lake Polly.

"Gotta be on the north end of the lake," Jeff said. "Shouldn't be a problem to find."

What my handmade map failed to disclose was the several little fingers and bays on the north end of the lake. The portage was likely at the end of one of these bays, but which one? We tried the first one. Nothing, so we turned around and canoed back to try the second bay, which was longer and had a big bend in it.

As we rounded the bend, much to our surprise, we suddenly came upon four young women sunbathing on a big rock out-cropping. When they spotted us, they all four jumped to their feet and stood in a row, facing us. The two on the outside held up a huge towel that came nearly up to the necks of the four of them. We waved and smiled. They waved and smiled.

"Looks like we interrupted a little nude sunbathing," Jeff said seriously, but grinning from ear to ear.

"Appears so," I said. "Keep paddling. Make it look like we know where we're going."

We paddled on, now not at all confident that this was the correct route to the portage. Later we decided that if it had been, the women would not have chosen what they considered an isolated place with no possible canoe traffic. We paddled to the end of the bay. No sign of a portage. No hint. Nothing.

We turned the canoe around and paddled back the way we had come. This time a little further from shore. Once more the young women jumped to their feet. This time they were not smiling.

"Hand me the binoculars," Jeff asked. "I want to make sure they were doing what we thought they were doing."

I handed him the binoculars.

"Well..." I said after a minute or two.

"They were," said Jeff, smiling as he handed back the binoculars.

We paddled on, and a half-hour later found the portage to Lake Koma.

"Some benefits from not having a decent map," Jeff said that evening when we laughed about the afternoon's misadventures.

Some Practical Concerns

What about journal writing on your computer and storing your journal writing in digital form? It may work for some people, but it doesn't for me. Since 1982, when I bought my first computer, I have used these devices for my writing. But not for my journaling.

How about talking into a recorder—the latest digital ones are smaller than a cell phone. Or what about using a smartphone app for recording journal entries? Both of these options can store enormous amounts of material, which can later be transferred to a computer. I don't use these methods either.

For my journaling, I write with a pen, and I write on acid-free paper in hardcover artist sketch books. I have a special elk leather cover that slips over the cover of the journal I am currently working with—this is probably my own little fetish, but for me, my journal is a very personal, special document.

I have found that writing with a pen is a profoundly different experience than writing at a keyboard. I can't explain why, but when I am writing with a pen on paper, there appears to be a connection between my mind and my subconscious that runs through my arm to my hand and the pen. I often experience what my 80-year old writing student experienced—her hand was moving so fast she had to go back to see what she wrote. The experience is mystical and magical and there is nothing else like it.

I have tried writing journal entries with my computer, and I have tried recording them as well—but the experience is not the same as when I write in longhand, with a pen, on paper.

Another practical question I often hear: "What will you do with these journals when you die? Do you want people to read some of the very personal, and the anger venting stuff that's in some of them?"

My answer, "When I'm gone, I don't care." My only hope is that someone doesn't destroy them. This may be my ego kicking in, but I believe they do contain some useful information (maybe) but certainly one person's perspective on what was going on in his life. I am now working on volume 40 of my journal collection. Some of the journals include but one year of writing; others have more than one year. Over the years these journals have proven to be invaluable for my writing—especially when I am writing personal stories and want to make sure I have dates, names, and places correct. Of course, going back to read my journals often prompts me to write new stories about events and people I haven't thought about for years.

PART III

Creating Your Story

7

Choosing Which
Stories to Tell

The two questions I most often hear from newcomers to my writing workshops are: "What do I write about?" and "How do I get started?" Here are
some prompts that my writing students have found useful in answering
those questions.

Growing-up Years

Many of my students want to write about their growing-up years; they've
been encouraged by their children and grandchildren to do so, but they
have difficulty deciding where to start. These prompts stir up memories,
and once the event or person is recalled, the stories usually follow.

Early Years (to age 12)

- **Describe your school in detail, including the floor plan. What are
  your favorite memories of when you were an elementary school
  student? What story do you remember most vividly about elementary school? Who was your favorite teacher? Why?**

When I was in eighth grade, I contracted polio and missed many weeks
of school. In those days, all eighth graders attending one-room country schools took a day-long examination at the county normal school (a
teacher training institution). Not passing the test meant the student could

not attend high school. The examination was held on a Saturday in May, where all eighth graders from Waushara County sat in one big room—scared to death.

I knew about this examination of course. As I was recovering from polio, unable to walk, I worried about failing the dreaded exam. Mrs. Jenks, my eighth grade teacher, was concerned about me passing as well. When I was well enough to be out of bed several hours each day, she stopped by with my lessons, answered any questions I had, took my written assignments with her to be corrected, and stopped by again the next day. She did this for several weeks until I was well enough to begin attending school again.

Even with her help, I was still nervous about taking the exam, an eight-hour agony of test after test. I need not have worried. Thanks to Mrs. Jenks and her daily visits to our farm, I passed with flying colors. I could attend high school.

- **What was your greatest fear when you were a child? Can you recall something that happened when you were especially afraid? Who or what was involved?**

- **What games did you play at school and at home? Any stories associated with these games?**

One of the favorite "games" my brothers and I played as kids was to mimic the *Tarzan of the Apes* radio show by grabbing the hay fork rope and swinging from one beam to the other in the hay mow of our cattle barn. As we swung across we would yell, "Tarzan of the Apps!" which seemed appropriate, as our last name was Apps. One day when we doing this, my brother Darrel made a mistake.

The barn beams were about fifteen feet from the floor. Darrel did not push off from the first beam enough so that he would reach the second beam, some twelve feet away. With only a small amount of hay on the floor and a lot of dust, there was nothing to break his fall if he didn't make it from one beam to the other.

Darrel grabbed the hay fork rope, yelled "Tarzan of the Apps," and then found he was hanging fifteen feet from the floor with no hope of reaching the opposite beam. My brother Donald and I stood watching in amazement. What will he do? Darrel had two choices. He could slide down the rope and suffer severe rope burns, or he could let go and chance not breaking something when he fell to the not-very-well-cushioned wooden barn floor. He chose the latter. With a huge thump, he landed on the small clump of hay, as a big cloud of dust surrounded him. When the dust cleared, I asked him if he was okay.

"I think so," he said as he slowly got to his feet. "But my side hurts."

We agreed not to tell our parents what had happened for fear they would put a kibosh on "Tarzan of the Apps." For several days Donald and I helped Darrel with his chores as he recovered from his fall. Years later, when Darrel was X-rayed for a different injury, the doctor discovered evidence of an earlier broken rib.

- **Do you remember when you learned to ride a bike? What were the circumstances?**
- **What was your favorite toy? What was your favorite book when you were a child?**

When I was about three years old, my mother made me a Teddy bear. She found the front and the back of the Teddy bear printed on a flour sack. She cut it out, sewed it together, and stuffed it with the same material that she used for making quilts. The little Teddy went wherever I went. I pushed it around in a toy wheelbarrow; I pulled it in my red wagon. I had other favorite toys but none as special as my little Ted.

When I was about three, my favorite books were the *Uncle Wiggly* series of children's books that my mother read to me. Later, the *Sears & Roebuck* catalog became my favorite book, for on those pages was everything a little boy would ever want. The catalog arrived in the spring and fall, with a special added Christmas "wish book" edition that arrived in November.

- **Describe Christmas or some other holiday important to your family. Recall a story when you were particularly happy, or one when you were particularly sad.**
- **Do you recall any trips you made with your family?**

As dairy farmers, any trip had to be close enough so that we could be home in time for the evening milking. Cows required milking 365 days of the year, so there were no vacations—no days away from the farm. Our day trips often meant visiting relatives. We had an unusual circumstance in our family—although perhaps not as unusual as I once thought. My mother did not much care for several of my dad's relatives; and my dad absolutely detested several of my mother's city relatives.

It was a cold winter day, a Sunday, when my dad decided we should stop by his older brother's farm for a visit. Uncle Ed lived on the poorest of poor sandy farms. He milked a few skinny cows, lived in a house that was never painted, had a passel of kids—my cousins—and barely scratched out a living. He and his sons were great hunters and fishermen—indeed they depended on wild game for much of their food supply. Uncle Ed was also a premier storyteller among storytellers. I enjoyed going to Uncle Ed's farm just to hear the stories—most of them about hunting and fishing and living off the land.

When we visited with Uncle Ed and my aunt Edith, they always insisted that we stay and eat. My mother worried about what we were eating. Would it be raccoon, squirrel, or maybe venison? The later two would be okay, as we ate a goodly amount of these wild meats at home as well. But my mother couldn't wrap her mind around the idea of eating raccoon.

When we arrived on that wintry Sunday afternoon, their wood burning cook stove had made their drafty old farm house warm and even cozy—at least that's how I remember it. I glanced toward the stove and off to the side, on some old newspapers lay a full-grown, dead raccoon. I was hoping my mother wouldn't see it. But she did. She didn't say anything, but when we sat down to eat I noticed that she only ate vegetables and passed on the meat. I knew she was thinking that another raccoon had made it into the stew pot—where the one on the floor was likely headed.

On the way home, she let my dad know what she thought about eating at Uncle Ed's farm.

"Herman, I'm not eating there again. I will not eat raccoon."

"I think we were eating squirrel stew, and besides, Ed's my brother. We'll eat there again."

And we did, but my mother didn't like it.

Teen Years (13–19)

- **What rules did your family have? Think of a time you broke these rules.**

In my book, *Every Farm Tells a Story* (Voyageur Press, 2005), I included a list of rules for doing chores. On our farm, my brothers and I each had chores to do each day. And there were rules for doing them. These rules were never written; we didn't know they existed until we broke one of them. But the rules for doing chores were critical and it was clear they should never, ever be violated.

Examples of rules:

- Perform your chores so well that you have the opportunity to move up to more challenging ones.

- Never complain about your chores, no matter what the weather or what else you would prefer to do at the time.

- Never miss doing your chores. (No one discussed the consequences of missing chores, because the imagined punishment was too frightful.)

- Feel free to brag about your chores when talking to your city cousins. (This was one of the few times bragging was permissible.)

- Describe your high school. What story or stories describe your good times there? The bad times?
- Who were your best friends? How would you describe them?
- What was your greatest achievement in high school?
- How did you learn to drive a car? Who taught you?
- What happened when you went for your driver's license?
- Describe your first love.
- Who were your idols? Your heroes?
- Did you participate in sports? Which ones?
- Describe your first job for pay. How much did you earn?
- What was your favorite music? Your favorite books?

Young Adult Years (19–25)

- Did you have schooling after high school? Do you remember any post-high school education stories?
- Did you serve in the military?
- What was your first full-time job? What was the pay? Describe the job.

In my writing workshops, one exercise I give my students is to write about is their first job for pay. Here is what one of my students wrote:

My First Job
by Kathy Heyse

Every college student needs a summer job and I was no exception. Of course, once one has a job, the trick is to keep it. The summer after my freshman year of college I searched until I finally got a job working in a drugstore.

My boss, Mr. Smith, was the owner of the store. He probably came up to just under my nose. Of course, I am fairly tall. He had totally white hair that was quite thick and a little curly, a ruddy complexion, a square face, and a square body to go with it. He never said too much, always coming straight to the point.

My jobs were varied, but the main part was working the cash register. Mr. Smith's wife, a short woman with dark hair and a pleasant smile, showed me the ropes for my first couple days of work. She worked when I didn't so she gradually turned me loose to do my job on my own.

One absolute must was being able to figure out the tax for a purchase without looking at the chart. The night before my first day on my own, I practiced and practiced so I knew I could do it. Actually it wasn't all that hard. The sales tax in Indiana at the time was 2% and no tax on prescriptions.

Unfortunately, each morning when I walked in through the employee entrance and past Mr. Smith's office door, he would call me in. "Kathy," he would growl, "you had a 50 cent over ring yesterday." Or on another day, "Kathy, you had a 28 cent under ring." Or the worst, "Kathy, you had a difference of $1.22." Now these don't sound like much today, but it was 1965, and a quarter was worth a lot more than today. Finally, "Kathy, you've got to get better at this or I'll have to think about getting someone else." Eventually I did get it right.

Then he bought a new, big, fancy cash register. He instructed both Mrs. Smith and me on how to use it. Instead of only having keys going up to the hundreds of dollars, this one could go up to the $10,000s. I was pretty sure we'd never go that high in the drugstore, but the register was faster and easier and just plain nicer.

The first morning after we began using the new register I was once again called into Mr. Smith's office. This time it was for a $300 over ring. My heart sunk. I was sure my job was over. And then an amazing thing happened. For the very first time that summer, Mr. Smith looked up at me and smiled. "Mrs. Smith had an $800 over ring."

- **Who were your best friends?**
- **Where did you live, and what was it like?**
- **What were your favorite books and music?**
- **How did you meet your mate?**

Formal Relationship or Marriage Years (20–30)

- **Where did you live? What stories do you have of your first year together? What was memorable? Are there things you would like to forget, but your partner won't let you?**

- Did either or both families involved not approve of the relationship?
- Did you have children? What stories are associated with the birth of your first child? Your other children?
- What rules did you establish at home?
- If you remained single during this time, describe your life during these years.
- What leisure-time activities did you pursue?

Early Career (20–35)

- What accomplishments are you most proud of?
- What are the toughest problems you faced? Pick one and write a story about it.
- Did you have any major problems in your home or family during this time?
- What is the most important thing that happened to you during this time?
- Did you change jobs or careers?
- Were you ever laid off from work?
- If you had children, what was your relationship with your children like during these years?
- What continuing education did you participate in?

Middle Years (35–65)

- Describe your relationship with your parents.
- If you had children, what were your feelings when they left home?
- Describe your relationship with your brothers and sisters.
- What were your hobbies in these years? How have they changed over the years?
- Did you participate in volunteer activities?
- What were the critical events that marked this period in your life?

Later Years (65 and Beyond)

- If retired, what stories do you have about retirement? And what feelings did you have at the time you retired?

- Where have you traveled? Are there places you want to return to? Places you never want to see again? What places are you looking forward to visiting?

- What health challenges have you faced?

- What are your proudest achievements?

- What volunteer activities do you participate in?

Additional Writing Prompts

- Did you or do you now have a special place in your life? Almost everyone has a special place they like to visit; some refer to these as sacred places.

- Was there a special person (people) in your life? This may be one or both of your parents, your spouse or partner, a favorite teacher, a religious leader, a mentor, or a friend who has made a difference in your life.

The following is a story that one of my writing students wrote about her father:

The Secret
by Sharon Galloway

I could hear loud, angry voices coming from the kitchen. I hated to miss any drama or secrets, so I was hiding behind a closed door in our formal dining room, hoping to hear what this was about. My mother, father, and oldest sister, Virginia, were all taking part in the exchange. Mom and Virginia sounded tearful, and their voices sounded both angry and apologetic. Dad was obviously very angry. There was no apology in his voice! Usually I enjoyed getting firsthand information, but that day I was beginning to feel afraid. Frightened that "my sin would find me out."

Virginia was a college freshman. The year was 1946 and fake fur coats were all the rage. My father had decreed that a fur coat was unnecessary attire for a college freshman, and what my father decreed usually became law with no chance of reversal. In a rare moment of opposition, my mother actually condoned Virginia buying the coat of her dreams, out of her own savings. Virginia agreed that it would be wise to leave the coat at school and choose another coat to wear when she was home for breaks. To my five-year-old mind, this was high intrigue, and I was thrilled that I had gotten in on the secret. I wouldn't have given it up for anything!

On a night that I remember clearly, I was home alone with Dad. This seldom happened, so after he had told me the only story he had been willing to tell me upon request (which involved three old men sitting around a fire smoking their pipes, and was repeated until I begged him to stop), I said, "I have a secret!" His response was to ask me what my secret was, but I was unmovable. I had no intention of violating the trust I had been given. After several minutes of trying to coax the secret from me, Dad played his trump and announced that he had a secret also. He said, "If you tell me your secret, I'll tell you mine." I really did try to stand firm, but another secret was irresistible. I was skeptical enough to insist that he promise he wouldn't tell who told him "the secret" before giving it up. With anticipation, I demanded he tell me his secret as promised. I knew I had been tricked when he whispered that his secret was that he loved me.

I soon forgot the whole episode, but then Virginia arrived home for Christmas break. The storm was not long in coming. I waited, with dread, for them to figure out that I was the one who told, but to my great relief that was never suggested.

At a family gathering many years later, someone mentioned the time when Dad had found out about Virginia's fur coat, and everyone had their own opinion about who had told. The consensus of opinions was that Dad's sister, Aunt Isabel, must have told. She was the only one outside the immediate family who could have known. At this time, I decided it was safe to confess. They were all dumbfounded. In all those years, Dad had told no one. Not even Mom knew how he had heard about the coat. As underhanded as his method of extracting "the secret" had been, he had been true to his word, thus protecting "my secret" for many years.

- **Significant moments: A birthday party. When you first saw an ocean. A special friend from elementary school. Your first love.**

These questions ought to shake loose some of the memories that have been untouched for years. In chapter 4, I discuss several other kinds of activities that may also help to jiggle your memories and bring back thoughts you long ago considered lost.

8

What Every Story Needs

Having taught writing workshops for more than forty years, and telling and writing my stories for even longer, I've come to believe a good story requires certain elements. A story takes the reader or listener beyond a mere description, a report of an event, or character sketch of an interesting person, touching us more deeply than those things can. A good story can evoke memories and generate laughter or tears, or even anger.

A story can be a powerful communication tool, and the following components help to make it so. First off, a good story generally includes the following components.

Beginning, Middle, and End

The beginning of a story grabs our attention, tells us a little of what to expect, and is sufficiently strong that we want to read or listen more. Here is a story I wrote about the picnic held at the end of the school year at the one-room country school I attended.

Softball Game with Fathers

Growing up on a farm, most of us never saw our fathers play. We had seen them work—seemingly all the time. The end of the country school year picnic was an exception.

Ma had been busy all morning preparing potato salad, baking a chocolate cake, slicing homemade bread for bologna sandwiches, stirring up a batch of grape Kool-Aid, and cutting a fresh lemon into the half-gallon jug. The teacher gave the same instructions each year: bring a dish to pass, silverware, and sandwiches enough for your own family.

The school picnic at our central Wisconsin one-room country school (Chain O' Lake) was a highlight for all the students; it celebrated the end of the school year. It also gave the students and their parents a chance to thank their teacher, and the teacher an opportunity to thank the parents for all their cooperation during the past school year.

Outside the bountiful potluck meal, my fellow students and I looked forward to the annual softball game between the students and their fathers. Few of the fathers had played softball since the previous year's game, whereas we kids played every day. Any student who wanted to play could—boys, girls, first graders on up. All the fathers also played, except for one or two with a bum leg left over from some farm accident.

This particular year, I was pitcher of our school's softball team (we played other country schools in the area beginning in April, when the weather warmed enough). Not to be boastful, but I was a fair to middling pitcher. At least, I had struck out some of the better batters from Willow Grove, one of the schools we played each year.

When Pa came up to bat, he spit on his hands like he did when he picked up a shovel or an ax. He hunched over the plate and stared at me as I stood on the pitcher's mound, which was more a sandy hole than a mound. Without putting it in words, his actions said, "Show me what you've got."

I let fire with my fastball—underhand of course—and Pa took a mighty swing. He missed and almost fell down.

"Strike one," Mrs. Jenks, our teacher and the umpire for the game, announced loudly. Pa's face turned red. He made ready for my second pitch.

"Hey, Herm," Bill Miller yelled. "Bat got a hole in it?" Pa acted like he hadn't heard, but his face grew even redder.

I wound up and this time slipped my slow ball across the outside of the plate. Pa took another mighty swing and the ball shot straight up in the air, about as high as one of the tallest oaks. Jim Kolka, the first baseman, walked over and stood where he knew the ball would fall and caught it easily.

"Out," Mr. Jenks said in her authoritative voice.

The game went on and as usual, the students won. I don't remember the score, but I do remember the wonderful time I had. When we got home I expected to hear something from Pa about how I had tricked him with my pitching. What he said, with a smile and twinkle in his eye, was, "You had a lucky day, Jerry. I didn't want to show you up by hitting a home run."

In my eyes, Pa had hit a home run just by playing the game, being a good sport, and taking his turn batting. And allowing me to see him play—something he seemed never to have time for on the farm in summer.

In shorter personal stories, similar to this one, the first line or two must capture our attention, and prompt us to continue reading or listening to the story or not. The beginning should tell us a little of what the story is about, and perhaps give us a hint of where the story took place and when. I tried to do that with the first three sentences of the country school story I shared above:

Growing up on a farm, most of us never saw our fathers play. We had seen them work—all the time. The end of the country school year picnic was an exception.

The middle is where you develop the story, each segment building on the previous and all leading toward the ending. In the ending you tie it all together, perhaps reminding readers of the beginning, leaving them feeling satisfied, entertained, informed, and maybe that they have learned more about you, the story's creator, and even more about themselves as readers or listeners of the story. I tried to do that with these final words:

The game went on and as usual, the students won. I don't remember the score, but I do remember the wonderful time I had. When we got home I expected to hear something from Pa about how I had tricked him with my pitching. What he said, with a smile and twinkle in his eye, was, "You had a lucky day, Jerry. I didn't want to show you up by hitting a home run."

In my eyes, Pa had hit a home run just by playing the game,
being a good sport, and taking his turn batting. And allowing
me to see him play—something he seemed never to have time
for on the farm in summer.

Characters

You are an important character in your story. But other people are important as well. These characters need to come alive. We must be able to visualize them in our minds, how they look, their mannerisms, what they wear
and how they talk. Some storytellers go to great lengths telling us about
characters in their story, to the point that we lose track of the story. Here is
a case where less is usually more. When we are told just enough about the
character so we can picture him or her in our mind, that's when it's enough.

My father figures prominently in many of my stories. He was a man
with limited formal education—his parents pulled him out of school after
fifth grade so he could go to work—yet he was able to make a living and
raise a family of three boys on a rather poor farm. He was proud of his
farming skills, the cattle he raised, and the crops he grew. But rather than
say that in so many words, the story below illustrates the point and goes
further in helping us learn more about him and his personality.

On a late August Sunday afternoon, a black 1938 Chevrolet
rolled up the driveway and stopped in front of our farmhouse.
Several kids piled out of the car, as did my mother's cousin and
her husband. They were city people. They lived in Wisconsin
Rapids, where the husband worked in the paper mills, as did his
father before him. The husband, Charlie was his name, knew
nothing about farming, and as my dad said, "He has no interest
in learning either."

After a little small talk, my dad asked Charlie, "Would you
like to see my pickle patch?" That year we had a half-acre of
cucumbers that we grew as a cash crop for a pickling plant in
Wild Rose.

Charlie rose up to his full five foot five, pushed his hat back
on his head, and said, "What you are calling a pickle patch is
more properly called a cucumber patch. They remain cucum-
bers until they are pickled."

Dad said nothing for a bit, then he looked Charlie right in the
eye without so much as a blink, and said, "Do you want to see
the pickle patch or not?" [10]

That exchange between Charlie and my dad said more than any description I could write about dad's personality and his attitude toward those he considered "know it alls."

Dialogue

Dialogue means people talking. It gives life and immediacy to your story. It helps move a story along, often contributing to the suspense. Dialogue also helps us see the characters (you as the storyteller are one of the characters, of course) in more depth.

Here is a story I wrote about four women going to visit Andy Meyer, the manager of a small local pickle factory, for my book *In a Pickle*. The dialogue tells us much about the characters' personalities, beliefs, and motivations.

That afternoon a newer blue Buick car pulled up to the pickle factory. Four big women wearing flowered dresses and hats piled out and walked single file from the car to the pickle factory steps. Andy saw them coming. They looked familiar— they were the same women he'd seen on the parade float trying to sing hymns. They looked like four big ducks waddling in a row, one right after the other. On a mission, looking for some answers.

One after the other they marched up the steps and across the factory floor to where the crew was working.

"I'm looking for Andy Meyer," the lead duck said. It was obvious that her feathers were ruffled.

"I'm Andy."

"My name is Prudence Wordsworthy of the Church of the Holy Redeemed. We need to have a talk." She did not extend a hand.

"Sure, go ahead."

"Can we talk privately?" Prudence asked. When she spoke she twitched so that the big colorful flowers on her hat vibrated.

"How about in the office?" Andy led the way, and the four women, still in single file, paraded behind him. It reminded him a little of his days in the army, when everybody walked in a straight line, in step.

Andy shut the door. He offered the two chairs in the office, but the foursome refused to sit, so Andy took the chair by the desk. The office was fairly bursting with heavily perfumed, big women.

"What can I do for you?" Andy asked.

"As I said, we are from the Church of the Holy Redeemed. You know about our church, young man?"

"Yes, I do," Andy answered. It was already getting warm in the little office, and the heavy smell of perfume was giving him a headache.

"I believe you know our beloved preacher, Arthur Ketchum?"

"Yes, I know him well. He's worked here all summer."

"Well, that certainly has been a mistake. He never should have sought outside employment. He should have said he couldn't make ends meet. The ladies of the church would have helped him out and made sure he got a few more potatoes, a half a hog, or an extra sack of rutabagas. We could have helped him out. He didn't need to work here."

"He turned out to be a good worker."

"That Helen Swanson worked here too, didn't she?" the head duck asked.

"Yes, she did," Andy said.

"She's been a member of our church for only a short time. What do you know of her background? Why did she get divorced? What did she do here? Why would a woman work in a place like this, anyway?" the head duck snarled.

"She is our bookkeeper, and a darn good one, too," Andy said, raising his voice a little.

"You watch your language, young man. There will be no coarse language in our presence."

"Sorry," Andy said, not sure what he had said that was considered coarse.

"We may have misjudged that Helen," the short duck hissed.

"That woman, that harlot," the lead duck sputtered. *"She's the one responsible for all this."*

"That's what happens when an upstanding church like ours accepts a divorced woman into its midst," the second duck hissed. She pulled a dainty handkerchief from her sleeve and dabbed her forehead.

"That Helen, she's the one responsible for all this," said the third duck, who had previously not spoken. She barely opened her mouth when she talked, so the words came out a bit garbled.

"Responsible for what?" Andy asked.

"You know full well. You know what was going on between that seducer and our spiritual leader. You knew what was going on," the lead duck chimed in as she wagged her long, crooked finger in Andy's face. *"Don't you know how to control your help? Can't you keep your employees in order and show them how to walk down a Christian path?"*

"Didn't think it was any of my business what path they chose."

"Well, it should have been your business. If you'd been doing your job, leading your people in the way of the Lord, this wouldn't have happened," the lead duck said in a too-loud voice.

"It's sad, so sad what this Helen did to our beloved preacher," the short duck said. She was shaking her head back and forth vigorously. Andy wondered if her big hat would remain in place.

"So sad," the second duck said.

"So sad," the third duck mumbled.

Just then came a loud knock on the office door, and Blackie Antonelli stuck in his head. *"Andy, where in hell are the extra pickle crates?"*

"Humph," the lead duck said as she bristled and ruffled her feathers. "You will not speak such words in the presence of Christian women," she huffed.

"Oh, sorry," Blackie said to the woman, whose face was red. He turned again to Andy. "Where in hell are the extra crates?"

"Back of the salt bin," Andy answered.

"Is he... is he an example of the kind of help you have here?" Prudence Wordsworthy was trying to catch her breath.

"Blackie's a good worker. Swears a little too much, but he works hard."

"How do you put up with having such a long-haired heathen in your midst? Oh, poor pastor. No wonder he strayed. No wonder he allowed the wiles of a dangerous woman to lead him off the path. Working around heathens every day. Oh, the poor man. The poor man, whatever has become of him? Whatever has become of him?" the lead duck asked.

"Oh, the poor man," the third duck mumbled.

"Oh, the poor man," the second duck added.

"Oh, the poor man," the little duck concluded.

To Andy it sounded like a barnyard chorus, with each big woman repeating what the previous one had just said." [11]

When thinking about writing dialogue for your stories, you might say, "I really don't remember the exact words my grandfather used to share his experience as a child growing up in the wilds of northern Wisconsin in the early 1900s, but I remember the gist of what he had to say."

In some cases, it is appropriate to create the dialogue as you would have imagined it to be. But there are some caveats. If your grandfather is in one of your stories, and you did not have an opportunity to interview him but you want to have him speaking, remember that your grandfather surely didn't talk as you do today. So if you have not been around old timers to capture their way of speaking, you may want to do a little research. One great place is a coffee shop where old timers gather for early morning coffee. Without being obtrusive, listen in. Capture the language that they use and how they use it, from sentence structure to word choice. For example, they might drop their gs, saying words such as *workin'* and *doin'*. They might use slang, such as *ain't,* and you might hear colorful phrases such as "Ain't that just a bugger," or "Oscar's wife has sure gotten fleshy," or "That new guy from Milwaukee just can't cut the mustard as a farmer."

Consider ethnic, regional, and educational background when creating dialogue. If your grandfather moved from Alabama to northern Wisconsin, he probably brought with him some of his southern dialect, so he would talk differently than those born and raised in Wisconsin. Someone with a German background will likely speak differently than someone with Asian roots. A character with limited formal education might speak differently than someone who has an advanced degree.

When I write my own stories, I often interview relatives and others who know about the story or the subject of the story. I always record the interviews, not only to make sure that I have a record of what the person said, but of the way in which the person said it. From these interviews I can often garner dialogue that I use in my stories. I know the dialogue is accurate, because I have a recording of the person's words. (This of course doesn't necessarily mean the person has all of his or her facts straight—you may want to later check the facts for accuracy.)

Dialogue is a powerful component of personal stories. People enjoy hearing what other people have to say and exactly the way they said it. Reading and listening to dialogue not only helps to move a story along and create suspense, but it also gives us additional insight into the person talking. Through dialogue, a person can reveal much about himself or herself.

Conflict

Stories have conflict. Nancy Lamb cites four basic types of conflict: Person against person, person against nature, person against society, and person against self.[12]

Our personal stories are generally filled with conflict, and as we write about the conflict, whatever form it might take, we provide suspense for our stories. Here is a story based on a memory of my first day of high school to illustrate conflict.

> *As a farm kid coming from a one-room country school to high school in the village of Wild Rose, I had heard stories of town kids making fun of and playing tricks on those "farm hicks" coming to high school from the farm.*
>
> *The year was 1947. After my first school bus ride, which took my fellow bus riders and me all around the countryside, we*

finally arrived at Wild Rose and the brick high school that I would attend for the next four years. I was both excited and anxious when I stepped off the red, white, and blue bus (it would be several years before school buses were yellow and black) and looked up at the building that housed the village grade school on the first floor and the high school on the second.

I walked up the creaky steps to the second floor, looking for the homeroom for the new freshman class. In the hallway, I met a student who was older and considerably taller than I was, and heavier too, likely a senior.

"Which direction is the freshman homeroom?" I asked.

"So you're a freshman?"

"Yes, I am," I answered.

"You look like a farm kid," the older student sneered.

"Well, yes, I am," I said quietly.

"We have a little game we play here in high school," the older kid said.

"I haven't got time; I don't want to be late on my first day."

"This game won't take but a minute," he said. He stood right in front of me, blocking my way.

"So, what's the game?"

"It's called hand wrestling." He went on to explain that you held up both your hands, spread your fingers, and the other guy entwined his fingers with yours. Then you tried to make the other guy kneel by squeezing his fingers and pushing down.

I did what he suggested.

"On the count of three, we begin," he said, smirking.

"One... two..." and he began squeezing my fingers and pushing down.

Before I had time to tell him he had cheated, he had both my hands pushed back and was squeezing hard on my fingers. I squeezed back and pushed and soon discovered that my fingers were much stronger than his. First a surprised look came over his face, then tears swelled in his eyes as he kneeled and said, "Stop, stop, you're hurting me."

I wanted to say that I assumed he had that in mind for me but I didn't. I also didn't tell him that I milked cows by hand twice a day, which resulted in strong hands and fingers. I made it to the freshman homeroom on time. And as the days and months passed, this bully never asked me to hand wrestle again.

Suspense

Suspense keeps us reading because we want to find out what happened. Unfortunately some would-be storytellers tell us what happened at the very beginning. They destroy the suspense and give the reader no incentive to keep reading, or keep listening, or watching, depending on the medium we are using for our storytelling.

I could have said at the very beginning of the modest little tale I told above that I bested a school bully on my first day of high school. By doing so I would have destroyed any sense of "What happened next?" which is what suspense is all about.

Here is a story one of my writing students submitted that illustrated well the concept of suspense.

A Day at the Brandt's
by Genevieve Brandt Kirchman

It was a warm summer's day and my brother, Paul, was target practicing in the yard. Today's target was a squirrel on top of our two-story house, but his keen eye and arrow-shooting skill failed him. The squirrel disappeared. Switching his attention, the day proceeded with the usual rhythm of summer in the 50s.

Until lunch. With nine children, our living room was "child friendly," which meant a linoleum floor, vinyl covered furniture and nothing of value. As Mom entered the living room, she heard a persistent scratching and squeaking from the fireplace. "Paul, come in here and see what's making the sound." Paul slowly opened the draft and re-encountered the squirrel from

*that morning. He DID hit it, but it had fallen into the chimney.
It was now clawing frantically, clinging to the brick wall and
losing its grip. It would soon be entering The Brandt World.
Paul quickly closed the flue and updated Mom.*

*Mom immediately yelled for my dad. "Merv, get in here right
away—we've got a problem." As Merv entered the living room,
he quickly surmised the problem—and the solution. Returning
in minutes from his office, he spoke deliberately and calmly.
"Paul, very slowly open that flue; everybody else, stand back."
Paul did as instructed, using the poker to hasten the squirrel's
descent. As soon as it hit the hearth, it tried to escape but the
linoleum was too slippery to get any traction. Merv then pulled
out the revolver he'd concealed behind his back and right there,
on the living room floor, it was over. As Merv returned to his
desk, he looked over his shoulder and said, "Paul, clean it up."
The rest of us stood there, somewhere between nonchalance,
dismay, and horror, depending on our gender. Just another day
in our family circus.*

Emotion

Stories can make us laugh, make us cry, sometimes make us angry, and
may include a combination of emotions. One way I judge whether I have
emotion in my stories is my reaction to my writing as I am writing. If the
story is supposed to be funny and I'm not chuckling when I'm writing, no
one is likely to laugh when they read it either. Likewise, when a story has a
sad moment, I'd better be tearing up when I'm writing or it's not likely to
have an emotional impact on the reader.

Emotion is what makes many stories memorable. It strikes deep at
what makes us human. Oft times in the first draft of a story, the emotion
may be merely hinted; a rewrite can often make it stronger. One time I
wrote about a memory of what my mother prescribed for those who had a
bad cold. Here is the first draft of what I wrote:

*When you develop a bad cold, ease the symptoms by drinking a
whiskey sling. Make a whiskey sling by pouring a shot of whiskey into a glass of hot water and adding a little lemon to make
the concoction go down easier.*

It's a memory that some readers might find interesting; indeed some
may have even experienced the same remedy when they were children.
In the revision I added one line at the end, *Repeat if necessary.* By adding
three words, the little piece now has a humorous twist to it. I've read this

little snippet to many audiences and it always draws a chuckle. "Laughter engages people," says documentary television producer Mik Derks. He adds, "But it's not just humor. I am looking for all the emotions. I'm looking for the passion... for what people are feeling about an experience." [13]

Details

Details give life to a story, make it interesting, and provide memory triggers for your audience. In the earlier story about the end of the school year picnic, almost everyone can identify with Kool-Aid and softball. Pa spitting on his hands. The pitcher's mound being a sandy hole, and so on.

Your audience wants to know what the weather was like when the story happened, the appearance of a building, how something tasted, how something smelled, the kinds of clothes someone was wearing, and more.

Barrington makes this point about the importance of details in storytelling: "...it is precisely in the particular details of one person's story that the writing opens itself up to its readers, allowing them to enter the story rather than stay at a distance, as they do when the writing is more abstract." [14]

But a story can become mired in details, to the point that it's stuck and the reader loses sight of the story. Details are essential to good storytelling, but knowing how many and which details to include is part of the art of storytelling. For instance, in describing a person, perhaps your father or mother, it is not necessary to go on and on about facial and body features, about personality quirks and speaking styles. Some of these characteristics are better shown through having the person speak—using dialogue in your writing. Or showing the personality of the person by having him or her doing something that illustrates that person's personality. Often mentioning one or two defining characteristics such as, "My father had big, calloused hands—the result of many years of hard physical work on the farm," is all that is necessary.

Here is an excerpt from a story that I wrote about a neighbor I became acquainted with when I was a kid. I used detail and dialogue to help the reader visualize a picture of this unusual man, who had both a serious speech impediment and a unique gift.

I remember the first time I accompanied Pa on one of those trips to Morty's place. I must have been four or five. It was a cold January day, the snow piled high everywhere. I could see a thread of smoke coming from the house's single chimney as we approached. We trudged up to Morty's kitchen door, and Pa knocked. Soon the door swung open, and I got my first up-close look at Morty Oliphant.

"Cuh... cuh... come in," he said in his halting way of speaking. To my surprise, Morty wasn't nearly as fearsome as some people made him out to be. True, his white hair seemed to fly off in every direction, his beard was long and scraggly, and his bib overalls and flannel shirt were faded from many washings. But he was obviously pleased to see us on this cold winter afternoon.

"How are you, Morty?" Pa asked, shaking his hand.

"Pr... pr... pre...etty good," Morty stammered. He offered us chairs by the woodstove. Pa and Morty talked and I listened, trying to understand what Morty was saying. Pa knew Morty well and was patient with him, waiting for him to say what he had to say, even though nearly every word was a struggle for him to get out.

After a few minutes, Pa asked, "You still got that pet raccoon? I'll bet Jerry would like to see him."

Morty made a clicking noise with his mouth and, to my aston-ishment, a full-grown raccoon stepped out of a wooden box in a far corner of the kitchen. It walked to where Morty was sitting and looked up at him.

"Ha... ha... ha...ow are you?" Morty said to the furry animal. The raccoon cocked its head to one side and made a purring noise, not too different from the sounds I was used to hearing our barn cats make. Morty and the raccoon were clearly com-municating.

Morty took an unshelled peanut from his pocket and handed it to the animal. The raccoon took the peanut in its paws, dropped it to the floor, and used its paws (almost like human hands) and its mouth to open the shell and eat the peanut.

"What do you think of that?" Pa asked me.

"It's really something!" I said. I had never seen a raccoon this close, and I had never seen one kept as a pet.

Morty offered the raccoon more peanuts, and soon there was quite a mess of peanut shells on the kitchen floor. With each peanut Morty would say something I couldn't make out, and the *raccoon would cock its head to the side and look right at him, making those purring sounds. After a bit, the raccoon walked back to its box in the corner. I sat there amazed at what I had just seen, but there was more to come.*

"Does that other critter still live under your house?" Pa asked, smiling.

"Ya... ya... ya-up," Morty said as he got up from his chair. He bent over and lifted up a loose floorboard.

I was absolutely astounded to see a full-grown badger emerge from its home under Morty's kitchen floor. Pa had always told me that badgers were vicious and that I should avoid them. But this one calmly followed Morty over to his chair as Pa and I watched. Then Morty and the badger carried on a conversation—at least that's how it looked to me. I couldn't understand a word Morty was saying, but the badger could. And likewise Morty seemed to understand what the badger's quiet growls and purrs were all about.

After that day, I was always eager to join my pa on a visit to Morty Oliphant's place. I continued to be astonished by how this humble man, so often shunned by people because of his speech impediment, could relate to wild animals in a unique way. His animal friends didn't mind at all that he couldn't speak clearly.[15]

Scenes

Stories are made up of scenes, in a fashion similar to a stage play, where the scenes are often identified in the program. In a stage play, each scene is a little story contributing to a larger one. I learned the importance of scenes in storytelling when I wrote my first children's picture book, which was based on a memory I had about growing rutabagas on our home farm... three acres of them, with more than three-hundred bushels harvested (*Eat Rutabagas*, Amherst Press, 2002).

In creating the book, I first wrote the story, not thinking at all about the illustrations that I knew would eventually be a part of the final product. The publisher asked that I meet with the illustrator to decide what illustrations should accompany the text. The artist, a delightful Swedish woman who had only recently come to this country, asked me, "How many scenes are in your story?"

I told her that I really hadn't counted them. So together we looked at the story and counted 20 scenes—little stories within the larger story. Each of the scenes in the story became an illustration for the book. For each scene, she asked me what the central point of the scene was—so she would know what to feature in the picture that she was painting. In a couple of instances, I said I didn't know what the central point of the scene was. Her advice? "Delete the scene."

For many storytellers, creating scenes comes naturally. We don't even think about it, but the scenes are there. Sometimes we don't have the scenes in the right order. I say more about this when I discuss revision and rewriting in chapter 11.

Time and Place

Those reading and listening to personal stories want to know where and when the story took place. In a story about my grandparents I wrote:

> *Grandpa and Grandma Witt lived but a mile from our farm if you went straight across the fields, about a mile and half if you followed the road. Their farm was even more hilly and stony than ours. The land included a gully large enough to bury several farm wagons and even a Model T Ford or two and leave nothing visible for those who drove up the long hill from County A, along the dusty road to the Witt Farm.*[16]

The description of the place is quite obvious, while the time for the story more subtle. Mentioning the Model T Ford places the story in the 1920s and 1930s, when Model T Ford cars were popular.

Similar to writing descriptions about the weather, people, and events, writing about time and place is best done in moderation. Too much information about time and place and the story loses its momentum. Always remember that *the story comes first*. All the words and sentences you write are to enhance the story.

Context

A few years ago, one of my publishers asked me to review a manuscript they were considering for publication about a man who grew up in the early 1900s, on a farm where he worked with horses and did not have indoor plumbing or electricity. His stories were captivating, but in my review of the manuscript I noted that everything was local, with little or no reference to a larger picture—to a context in which the story took place.

I volunteered to write a foreword for the book, where I wrote about the larger picture by describing farming in the Midwest during the years of his story.[17]

Our stories often require context. If we are writing about something that we remember happened to us during World War II—the reader needs to know a little bit about that war.

For example, I remember eating lots of sorghum during World War II because my mother couldn't buy sugar. The reader may not know why my mother couldn't buy sugar—the answer? It was rationed, along with tires, gasoline, meat, canned food, and much more.

Context helps readers know how our story fits into a broader picture. Here is where you, as the storyteller, may need to do some research. See chapter 5 for some tips on how to do it. A word of caution: Everything in moderation, including the writing of context. I've known some storytellers who become so intrigued with the context for their stories that it gets in the way of the story. As important as context is, a little goes a long way.

Shows More Than Tells

A good story is told in such a way that your audience can see in their own minds what is going on. They can visualize the characters and can as a result feel a part of the story. It is as if the reader is standing by your side or looking over your shoulder when you are telling the story.

What separates a story from an essay, a news article, a letter to the editor, or a live lecture filled with long lists of facts and information, is that a story "shows" to get its point across rather than "tells." A good example of "telling" is a person who stands in front of you with a Power Point presentation. On the screen flashes a series of "talking points" that vibrate in multiple colors and are lined up showing one boring item after the other.

Several years ago, when I directed a national leadership development program for higher education middle managers, I took our group of thirty participants on a Missouri River canoe trip from the Garrison Dam in North Dakota, to Bismarck. We had spent a week living with the Mandan Indians on their reservation, and I invited a Mandan shaman to travel with us. Each evening, as we camped on the banks of the Missouri River, the shaman shared the creation stories of his people.

He was a great storyteller, and had a wonderful sense of theater as we sat around the blazing campfire on a cool June evening, with the river hurrying along just a few yards from where we had erected our tents.

I asked him to talk about the history of his tribe and their cultural practices. Earlier he had told me about the power of a vision quest, and I asked him to share that information with the group. Rather than beginning by talking about what a vision quest is, he showed us, with the following story:

> *I went out by myself for four days to a secluded place. I did not drink or eat anything, nor did I sleep. I prayed constantly, hoping to see a vision. On day four, I remember seeing two eagles sitting some distance from me with one coming toward me. This happened in the early morning before the sun came up. The meaning of this, as I understand it, is that I now have "eagle medicine."*

Here is an example of a draft I wrote, followed by a revision in which I tried to turn telling into showing. My mother was at St. Agnes Hospital in Fond du Lac, some seventy-five miles from our farm. She had traveled to the hospital with an aunt by train, and a week later my dad, brothers, and I visited her there for the first time.

In my first draft I wrote, "Upon arriving at the hospital, my father was angry when the nurse said my brothers and I could not see their mother in her hospital room."

Here's what I wrote in the revised version:

> *We walked up to the reception desk and the Sister asked how she could help. Pa said that we were there to see Mrs. Apps. The Sister looked through some papers and gave us the name of the room.*

> *"But no children are allowed to visit patients," she said.*

> *Darrel's lower lip started to quiver.*

> *"I want the boys to see their ma," Pa said with a firm voice. He put both of his huge hands on the desk and looked the Sister in the eye.*

> *"I think we can make an exception this once," the Sister said, smiling at me and my brothers.*[18]

Multiple Layers

Your personal stories have multiple layers. At one level, they inform. Your audience will learn something they may not have previously known. At another level a good story entertains—they are simply fun and a pleasant break from what is happening in a person's everyday life. Whether you want this to happen or not, your personal story reveals a good deal about you, the storyteller—what is important to you, how you see the world, and so on. At a deeper level, as you share your personal stories, they can cause your audience to recall their stories and to begin thinking about them and their meaning.

Sometimes you might not be aware that your story has multiple layers. Here are the last few paragraphs of a story I wrote about a Christmas Day shortly after World War II, when I was a youngster. Years after writing it, I learned that for some readers the story exemplified the true meaning of Christmas. I did not have that in mind, at least not consciously, when I wrote the story, which I intended to be a description of rural poverty and how neighbors looked after each other.

> *Later that afternoon, my brothers and I walked to the Davis farm, about three-quarters of a mile north of our place. Alan Davis and his adult daughter, Kathryn, lived in a ramshackle, paint-wanting house with no conveniences whatsoever. Most everyone in our community was poor in those days, but Alan and Kathryn had next to nothing—including, in Ma's judgment, often not enough to eat. Ma always baked an apple pie for them on Christmas and had us boys take it to them along with a small Christmas gift—that year a frilly handkerchief for Kathryn and a new pair of work gloves for Alan.*
>
> *The Davises welcomed us in, took our coats and caps, and sat us down by their wood stove. As they opened their presents, we looked around and saw that they had no Christmas tree or decorations—no sign at all that it was Christmas.*
>
> *"Tell your Ma thanks," Alan said.*
>
> *"Tell her thanks for me, too," said Kathryn. As she held up the handkerchief, I saw that she had tears in her eyes.*
>
> *I've never forgotten how thankful they were for the simple gifts we gave them, or their joy in having my brothers and me visit them on what must have been a lonely Christmas Day. Pa often reminded us that we all had a responsibility to look after our neighbors—especially on holidays, but every other day as well."* [19]

Theme

Theme refers to the central message—some might say the moral—of the story. Including a strong theme is one way to ensure that are telling a meaningful story rather than stinging together a rambling set of memories.

In the story I wrote about the end-of-school softball game, the theme is about the rare opportunity to relate to my father in a different way than we did during our everyday work together on the farm, and what that meant to me. The theme of the Christmas story above is how farm neighbors cared for and helped each other, especially during difficult times.

Total More Than the Sum of the Parts

In my many years of teaching, I have had several students who were good "mechanical" writers. They attended to all of the components. Yet their stories lacked the spark and excitement that make stories stand out—that "something" which makes a story special.

Unfortunately, there is no good way to describe what this something extra is that tips a story from being a reasonable one that follows all the guidelines, to becoming a story that goes beyond and becomes great. This is some of the mystery of creativity in storytelling. Simply following the guidelines does not necessarily a great story make. But, on the other hand, a great story generally has all the components that I have discussed, and something more that goes beyond the sum of the parts.

Sometimes, as I dig deeper into my own memory, I discover snippets of details, impressions of people, lines of dialogue, and more that can contribute to making a story more than merely a good story. It is this mystery of creativity that rests within each of us that can make a good story a great story. Often it is in the rewrite process that a story's "specialness" emerges. I'll say more about this in chapter 11.

9

Tips for Writing Your Story

Now that we've covered the components, or building blocks, of good stories, here are some tips on how to put them all together.

Ultimately, no two storywriters follow the same writing approach. What is most important is getting the story down on paper—not the approach you use for writing it. In my writing workshops, I tell students that the suggestions I offer are the ones that work for me. As they write their stories, they will discover the approach that works best for them.

Select a Point of View

The point of view of a story is the perspective from which the story is told. For writers of personal stories, I recommend using the first person perspective. Write, "I did this, I saw that, etc." First person writing represents the person speaking.

Occasionally I will see personal stories written in third person. Let's say the writer's name was George. He might write, "George and his father never got along, but George was able to accomplish much in spite of his father's stern ways."

As a reader, you immediately wonder who George is. Besides the confusion, third person writers of personal stories convey a kind of aloofness when they are talking about themselves in third person. Occasionally,

I see a personal story writer using the words, "This writer…" Why not avoid all the confusion and come right out and say "I."

"But my writing ends up sounding like 'I, I, I' especially if I start every sentence with 'I,'" my students say to me. So don't begin every sentence with "I." Vary the sentence structure. For instance, when talking about the place where you grew up, you might write, "I grew up in Long Creek, Minnesota," or you could say, "In Long Creek, Minnesota, my family had little to eat during the Depression years, but I remember doing many fun things. Sometimes I climbed trees, or played in the creek, or just sat on a hillside watching the clouds roll by."

Avoid using second person writing when storytelling. Second person writing usually begins with the pronoun "You," and represents a thing or a person being spoken to. Suggestions or commands often are cloaked in second person writing. In this book, I use second person writing on occasion—when making a suggestion about something you should consider doing. But when I am writing my stories, I do not use second person writing.

Avoid Flowery Language

When I read a piece of writing, whether it is fiction or nonfiction, and the writer gushes on about something or someone paragraph after paragraph. I want to grab the writer by the collar and say, "What happened to the story?"

Strunk and White, in their classic little book, *Elements of Style,* write, "Prefer the specific to the general, the definite to the vague, the concrete to the abstract." [20] Tell your story with simple sentences in everyday language. Trying to impress your audience with your vast vocabulary and your skill in creating long sentences and densely constructed paragraphs will only detract from your telling. It is your story that people want to hear, not your skill in using esoteric language. Tell your story in easily understood language so your audience doesn't have to think, "What'd he just say?"

One way to avoid flowery language that bogs down your writing is to avoid excessive use of adjectives and adverbs.

I remember getting carried away once when I was writing about a thunderstorm. In an early draft I wrote, "I awakened to the frightening, growling, trembling, animal-like sound of distant thunder. Looking to the southwest I saw jagged flashes of cold light cutting across a black, menacing sky where the clouds rolled and tumbled and tore into each other."

I revised the paragraph to read: "I awakened to the sound of distant thunder like a wild animal growling. Crawling out of bed, I glanced toward the southwest and saw flashes of lightning tearing across the ever blackening sky. Pa was right, rain was on the way."

Listen for the Whispers and Look in the Shadows

My father taught me to not only pay attention to what was going on in the world and what everyone was talking about—sometimes shouting about—but that I should also learn to listen for the quiet voices. Voices that are often not heard in the midst of all the yelling. Often, he said, it is the quiet voices that help one learn the depth of a story, or sometimes even the true story that all the shouting sometimes obscures. Same with looking in the shadows. My father would say, "There is more to see in the world than just that which is well lighted. Oft times, it is in the shadows where exciting things exist, out of the glare of bright light."

I try to follow his advice when writing my stories, pushing myself to remember things more deeply, to ask more probing questions when I interview people, to dig more deeply into background material so that I can capture some of what the whispers have to say and what is going on in the shadows.

Make the Ordinary Extraordinary

What I often do in writing my stories is begin with something very ordinary. As I write, I hope to make this ordinary thing or person much more than that. I hope to make the ordinary, extraordinary.

Here's a passage I once wrote about the seemingly common and ordinary woodpile:

> *In our farming community when I was a kid, a big woodpile made a statement. It said of the farmer, "I'm ready for the worst kind of winter." Woodpiles also demonstrated neatness and attention to detail—important values for any rural person, but especially important for farmers. Pa would often say, "Just look at Severson's nice woodpile."*
>
> *A translation of nice suggested first that Severson had a big woodpile, not a little dump of sticks, but a great pile of blocks as high as the tallest man in the neighborhood and as long as a chicken house.*
>
> *A second meaning of nice was the way the blocks were piled on top of one another, end to end with split sides showing. Severson's woodpile was the kind that people noticed and talked about; it made the Seversons stand out among the neighbors and gave them a place of prominence in the community.*

Engage All the Senses

Sometimes as writers we seem to forget that not only do we hear things and see things, but we also can taste, smell, and touch things. I remember when I gave my editor the manuscript for my first book. I was writing about my farm and I selected, rather cleverly I thought, a big, old black willow tree as one of the main characters. I called the tree the End Willow, as it was the first in a long string of trees that formed a windbreak for our farm's buildings. I described the tree's scraggly branches and how the western winds had cracked off some of them, leaving stubs. I mentioned how the old tree leafed out each spring, year after year. I wrote about its appearance in winter, spring, summer, and fall. I thought I had done a reasonable job of describing that old black willow tree.

Several weeks later, I met with my editor. When I asked what he thought about the End Willow, he quietly said to me, "You really don't know that old tree very well, do you?" I was taken aback. I thought I had described it quite well.

My editor went on, "I want you to tell me how the bark of that old tree felt when you ran your fingers over it. I want to hear the sound of the wind tearing through the dead branches in winter. I want to know what the leaves smelled like in May, when they first emerged and what they smelled like in October, when they fell on the ground."

It's a lesson I have never forgotten as I try to incorporate into my writing as many of the senses as I can—and doing it in such a way that my readers can experience what I am sensing as they read my stories.

We often overlook smells in our writing, failing to realize how powerful they can be not only in evoking emotion, but also in triggering memories for our readers. When I was a kid, the bakery in Wautoma, Wisconsin sent out a bakery truck loaded with sweet rolls, doughnuts, breads of various kinds, cookies, and more to the many farms in the area.

When the bakery truck arrived at our farm, the driver would back up to the kitchen porch and open the back door so that my brothers and I could see and smell the wonderful array of goodies he had to offer. My mother, a wonderful cook and baker in her own right, would look at what the "baker man"—as my brothers and I called him—had to offer. I don't recall that she ever bought anything, but the baker man stopped by once a week anyway.

Many years later, when I was working part-time for a book company in New York, I would fly into New York the night before meeting with my bosses. I am an early riser, so before the meetings, I would walk in Manhattan, taking in the sounds, sights, and smells of the big city. When I would come to one of the many little bakeries, I would smell the tangle of freshly made baked goods and exhaust smells of city traffic—and my mind immediately returned to the baker man who visited our farm so many years before. In my mind I could picture the bakery truck, the baker man, my mother, brothers, and myself. Then, too, there was the mixture of exhaust from the bakery truck with the baked goods he was carrying.

Create Rhythm in Your Writing

For a couple years a classical musician from a Minneapolis orchestra enrolled in my writing class. I probably learned as much from him as he learned from me. He helped me see how a written story and a good piece of music compare. One of the keys to good music, he explained, is rhythm. Rhythm is the flow of the music, sometimes quick, sometimes slow. It is the combination of sound and silence to create a beat—a pattern. Rhythm in music can relax us or excite us as it moves along. In addition, great music draws us in with a strong or intriguing beginning, and often ends with a satisfying conclusion. It often surprises us, and it touches us emotionally.

Everything my music-writing student said about good music applies to writing as well. One of the best ways to judge rhythm in your writing is to read it aloud and listen for how the words and sentences flow together, the high points and the low points, the moments of calm and the moments of excitement.

You can control your story's rhythm by varying the length and the structure of sentences. Include the occasional sentence fragment—even if your English teacher said it was a no-no. Occasionally use a series of short sentences, which speed up the writing. Then slow things down with a longer sentence. Begin sentences in a variety of ways. Sometimes begin a sentence with a preposition; or with a "but" or an "and." Variety in sentences can help the rhythm of a piece of writing. Sometimes repeat key words, as I repeated "walking" in the piece below, which is excerpted from one of my recent weekly blogs:

> *Out of the cold, late March gloom on a rainy afternoon, the deer came. Single file. Walking with heads down. Seven of them. Walking slowly through the slush and snow. Walking along my driveway a hundred yards from my cabin. Looking for spring. Big deer first, then mid-size ones, and finally a little, skinny one in the rear. All walking slowly. Survivors of a long, cold winter. Hoping they will once more find something to eat on this cold, rainy day with spring on the calendar, but yet here.*

Be Honest

Be honest. Write about things as they happened, not as you wished they had happened. Some things you may wish to leave out, but be honest about what you include.

In my week-long writing class one year, one of my writing students, a man in his sixties, turned in a manuscript that described his family. As I read the piece, I concluded that this was the most unusual family I had ever read about. His mother and father always got along. The kids were near perfect. Everything about the family was positive and upbeat. When I returned the manuscript to the person I commented that his family was one of the most perfect families I had ever read about.

He said, "Oh, we weren't all that perfect a family. I thought I should just write about the good things."

Families are not all joy and happiness. They reflect the human condition, which has its peaks and valleys, its high points and lows. It is this mix that makes us human. Thus we should not avoid, nor be ashamed of writing about, the valleys when we sometimes would prefer to only write about the mountaintops of our experiences. It is the truth of our telling that reveals who we are, what we believe, and what we value. When we truthfully tell our stories, including the sadness and disappointments as well as the successes and joys, we strip away the façade that we sometimes show the world, and show our real self. In doing so we sometimes feel naked as a jaybird. Putting it all down in writing makes for better stories, and may make us feel better as well.

Avoid Family Feuds

Only you can avoid a family feud over skeletons you do or do not unearth. Often in my writing classes students will ask, "What do I do about Uncle Charlie, or Aunt Mable?" They go on to explain in some detail what a reprobate their Uncle Charlie was—and then, usually with a smile, state that he was also so darn interesting. Same for Aunt Mable. "Rumor was that she spent some time as a prostitute."

I leave the decision to write or not write about these family members to the writer. I explain what I do with my stories when I am confronted with writing about an "interesting" person. The first question I ask: "Are there close descendants of this person still living in the area? Do you want to avoid embarrassing them?"

I faced a challenge when I wanted to write about the neighbors in the farm community where I grew up. To put it mildly, they were profane. Every member of the large family cussed, from the little four year old to his older brothers and parents. They cussed in every sentence. I often wondered if they were to cease cussing, would they have anything to say.

The problem for me was a couple of the boys still live in the community, along with their children. And today they are well respected and accepted. In writing about the family, I changed the family's name. I wanted to talk about them because they were so interesting, and provided such a contrast to our other neighbors, but I also didn't want to embarrass the family members still living in the community.

Sometimes you will write about a family member, but not include all the details about that person. Ultimately, writers have to decide for themselves how much to say. It can be a bit of a tricky question, but a question that must be faced.

When, Where, and with What

Some people find their creative juices flow best at midnight, for others it's early in the morning. I have the luxury these days of being able to write full time—it's my day job. But when I had a different day job for many years, I wrote every morning starting at 5:30 for a couple of hours. It's surprising how much work one can turn out with but two hours of writing per day, five days a week.

As for how I may develop a particular topic for a story I am working on—I create this in my head on my early morning walks. I write every morning, so when I return from my walk, with my mind map as a guide, and my mind fresh with new ideas from my walk, I am set for my morning writing.

Some of my students write with pen and pencil, others are comfortable at their computer keyboard. I learned to type in high school, on a manual typewriter. As technology improved, I learned how to write on an electric typewriter. Using an electric typewriter took some re-learning, as a manual typewriter requires a heavy touch and an electric typewriter merely a gentle caress. During the transition from a manual to an electric typewriter, all kinds of stray letters appeared in my writing, as my fingers rested where they shouldn't have. I learned how to use a typewriter eraser, and then the wonderful stuff called "whiteout" came along and I could smear a little of it over a letter I didn't want and type over it. Next was an electronic typewriter, a huge electric typewriter that had enough memory to remember a line of typewriting, so if you made an error, you could correct without having to use correction fluid. In 1982, I purchased my first "real" computer, a Kaypro. It cost $1800, and was advertised as portable. It "only" weighed 29 pounds and operated with two 5 ¼ inch floppy disks, with the software on one disc and the files on the second.

I've had a series of computers since then, but I still write some of my material in longhand. I write in longhand in my journal, and as I explained earlier, I keep a special notebook for each project that I work on and in it I write in longhand.

I advise my students that their writing will be easier if they can find a place that they can call their writing place—a desk in the dining room, a spare bedroom made into an office. A place where their work can be spread out and will remain undisturbed when they are away from their writing. Some students tell me that they do just fine writing at the kitchen table, or in an airport lounge in Dallas, or in a hotel room in Minneapolis in between meetings, or on an airplane headed for Anchorage. I have done considerable travel in my career, and have learned to write in all of these places, but not everyone can do that. Discover the place or places that work best for you.

I've been in this story writing business since the mid-1960s, and I have discovered that my favorite and most productive places for writing are where I can work for three or four hours a day without being disturbed, with no phone ringing, no emails wanting my attention, no one knocking on my office door. So I do considerable writing at my farm in central Wisconsin, where I work in a century-old granary that we have remodeled but continues to be heated with a wood stove, and where Wi-Fi has not yet found its way.

To Outline or Not

The common advice for many years and continuing today is "No matter what it is you want to do; you must first take time to plan." You may have also heard the slogan, "Plan your work; work your plan." This admonition of course became a part of storytelling, especially when writing personal stories.

Here is where personal style and preference play an important role. I know people engaged in writing personal stories who spend hours, sometimes days, creating elaborate outlines of what they will write. Many of them, especially those who were schooled in the 1970s and before, recall vividly the proper way to create an outline. It went like this:

I. Main Topic
    A. Subtopic
        1. Details about A
        2. Details about A
    B. Subtopic
    C. Subtopic
  II. Main topic

Some of the rules suggest every topic must have at least two subtopics, and every subtopic must have at least two subtopics. This is a very cut-and-dried approach to figuring out the details of the story you want to write, and determining what parts of the story are of most importance (main topics), and which contribute to main topics but are not main topics themselves (sub topics.)

I know writers who do no outlining at all—they merely write and let the story take whatever form that may evolve. They say, and I agree with them on this point, that too much pre-thinking, too much planning and outlining, can suck the creative juices out of a story, leaving it stale, mechanical, and often boring. The down side of the no-outlining approach is the need for considerable rewriting—which is not all bad, of course. Some of the "no outline" writers, and I am one of them on occasion, create an outline of their work when they have completed the project. In this way the outline becomes a guide for the revision.

Personally, I come out somewhere in the middle of the formal outline/no outline dichotomy. You will recall the mind mapping strategy that I described in chapter 4, and my suggestion that it can be an excellent way of accessing memories about a particular event, place, or person whom you are trying to recall from your past. Mind mapping can also be used as an outlining strategy for your stories.

A fundamental difference exists between mind mapping as an outlining tool compared to developing a formal outline like I described above. Formal outlining is a linear process, meaning you start at the beginning, and in a step-by-step fashion write down the topics and subtopics that you will include in your story. Mind mapping is a nonlinear approach to outlining. You start in the middle by indicating the story topic you want to write about, and in spiderweb fashion, you move out from the middle in all directions, indicating with circles the main features of your story. Each group of circles surrounding the middle circle will have additional circles that expand on and provide detail relating to the first group of circles.

I find this approach to outlining more useful and less mechanical than the formal approach, because not only can I see main topics and subtopics represented by the circles, I also can see how all of the parts of the story relate to each other. Also, there is plenty of room for creativity in writing the story, because what I have in my mind map is a skeleton of what the story might eventually look like. Very often in the process of writing the story, I will discover other topics that I remember and include them.

Project Notebooks and Notecards

For each writing project I work on, I have a project notebook. In some ways it's a special kind of journal that I keep for each project. From an office supply store, I buy college-ruled Composition Books. They have 100 lined pages, which is usually sufficient for how I use the project books. I also have a ready supply of 3 x 5" notecards that I try to carry with me at all times. When I'm hoeing in my garden, hiking in the woods, about to go to sleep at night, ideas flash into my mind and I scratch them down on my notecards. Sometimes I also write ideas directly in my project book, or I transfer them from the notecards to the project book, where I usually expand on the idea. When I think of a resource person, an article, or a book, or something I may have read on the Internet, I jot down the reference. If I am writing a book of stories, which is what I do fairly often these days, I write my sketchy outline, which is usually merely a list of topics I want to write stories about, or a mind map in the project book. As I write, the outline—which becomes a table of contents for the book—almost constantly changes as the book progresses. My project book is a record of these changes and when they occurred.

When I am writing fiction, I use the project book to record each character from the novel, his or her physical description, date of birth, date of death if deceased, any pertinent personality quirks, and the relationship of this person to other characters in the story. I also create for each of my characters a brief family tree, listing the names of parents and their birth and death dates.

When writing fiction, an all-too-common error is to not keep track of the physical characteristics of your characters. For instance, in chapter 2, a character has brown hair, in chapter 10 he is bald.

In my project book I also record all the place names that appear in the novel, and their characteristics, as well as the background information that I blend into the writing—the kind of weather in July, the crops grown by farmers where the story takes place, and other information that may be relevant to the story. There is nothing more jarring to the reader than to discover that Niceville or whatever you call a town has a population of 200 in an early chapter and discover that 2,000 people live there five chapters later. Readers like details, whether you are writing your story as nonfiction (which most of you will do) or as fiction. But in either case, the details must be as accurate. Here is where far-ranging research comes in handy— much of which I note in my project books. In the story I wrote about how to drive a Model T Ford car, (see chapter 5) I needed to make sure when Model T Ford cars were built, what they looked like, and how they were operated.

Additionally, I note the progress I am making in my project book. I am a firm believer in writing a story all the way through, whether it is 500 words or 50,000 words. The former you can probably write in one setting, the latter may take several weeks. In either case, I note in my project book the number of words I complete on a particular day. My books are written under contract with a publisher, where I indicate the approximate number of words the book will contain.

After each writing session, I also note the percentage of the project that is completed. I do these for several reasons. Noting the number of words completed, and comparing that number to the number of words required, helps me not to get lost in my story, meaning I avoid going off on a tangent. By checking words completed and knowing how many words I have left and how many topics still need attention, I can generally keep on track. During the revision process, I will obviously pay much more attention to such matters.

Noting the number of words written each day helps me to realize that I am indeed making progress on a writing project, even though some days I feel completely bogged down, despondent, and ready to abandon the story I am working on. By looking at the words already written, I can assure myself that some progress has been made, even though I may not think so at a particular moment when the words seem to be stuck somewhere between my brain and the keyboard.

Just Write the Story

Although it may sound paradoxical, I tell my students to not think about anything other than the story they are concentrating on writing, and not worry about the components when writing the first draft. I try to help them understand that as storytellers, the more stories they write and tell, the more the components will become second nature, and that the ideas will become embedded in their minds in the same way that they don't think much about spelling or where to put a comma or period. The important thing, I tell them, is to get the story down.

During the revision process they can examine in depth such things as scenes and their order, the beginning, middle, and end and other components that can improve the writing.

Too often students in my writing classes worry about their writing style. They have read about the writing styles of such notables as Hemingway or F. Scott Fitzgerald or John Steinbeck or some other well-known writer. I've heard my students say, if only I could write like one of these authors or some other author they mention. I tell them to keep reading, classics as well as contemporary stories, but don't worry about trying to emulate the style of a particular author.

As you write your story, just relax, be yourself, and let the words flow. Your writing style will emerge—without you even knowing it.

10

Overcoming Blocks

I have heard many reasons why workshop participants haven't written their stories: "I've just been so busy"; "I've started, but writing my stories is more difficult than I thought it would be"; "My memory is just not good anymore. I simply can't remember what it was like when I was a kid."

Other reasons for not writing have included, "Who would be interested in my story?"; "I'd do it, but I just don't know how to begin"; or "My world is filled with interruptions, the phone is ringing, the kids are yelling, my spouse has something for me to do, the Internet beckons and I am behind on answering the emails I received this week."

And a reason I sometimes hear, "I will write my story when I figure out the meaning of my life." This reason is one of the most baffling. On the one hand it suggests the person has been stumbling through a life with no meaning—a rather sad situation. The comment also illustrates the person's lack of knowledge of one of the great benefits of personal storytelling. The telling of one's story can be a powerful way for a person to find deeper meaning in their lives.

All of these reasons came from people who had enrolled in my writing class, where they intended to learn how to write their personal stories. In their defense, a number of these workshop participants were encouraged by a family member to attend my workshop, and in many cases, someone else—generally a family member—even paid their way to attend. They were in my workshop because someone else wanted them to be there.

Some of the very honest ones, despite the backing of a family member, would say, "I don't know why I'm wasting my time and your time in this class. This is not something that I'll ever do." I thanked them for their honesty, and took their comments as a challenge.

I don't argue with people about their excuses for not writing. I try to answer some of their concerns by telling my story (surprise). I shared that when I was teaching at the university, and my wife and I had three little kids that demanded a considerable amount of our time and energy, and I had as many as a fifty to a hundred university students enrolled in my classes that required me to read examinations, term papers, and all the rest connected with teaching, I had little extra time. So I made extra time. I would get up at 5:30 in the morning, and spend two hours at my typewriter—no computers in those days—writing my stories. Two hours a day, five days a week, meant ten hours a week, and ten hours a week times four weeks added up to forty hours, and if I only created three or four hundred words a day—sometimes fewer, sometimes more—by the end of a month I had a sizable pile of typewritten pages.

If you are motivated to get something done, you will find time to do it. For some it may be in the middle of the night, for others early in the morning—or whatever time a person can carve out of a busy day. The important thing is that the writing is done each day.

Occasionally a writing student will say something along these lines, "I want to pick up some tips on writing so when we go on vacation next summer I'll be able to devote some time to writing my stories." That plan almost never works. In my experience, it is far more productive to write a little everyday than try to write a lot in a few days—especially when the person is supposed to be enjoying a vacation with his or her family.

As to the excuses related to poor memory, see chapters 4, 5, and 6, where I discuss several approaches for getting in touch with your memories. Almost everyone can remember a lot more than they thought they could.

Procrastination

Procrastination blocks many writers. Here are some reasons I've heard as to why would-be writers procrastinate:

- "I'm concerned what people will think of my writing."
- "I've been waiting for the muse, then I'll begin writing."
- "I am a very busy person—when am I supposed to find time for writing?"
- "I must confess, I don't use my time wisely—in fact, time really gets away from me."

To overcome procrastination:

1. Admit to yourself that you have a procrastination problem. Realizing that you have a problem is the first step to overcoming it.

2. Decide on a time to write, even if it may only be a half hour a day. Mark it on your calendar and stick to it. If you are sitting at your desk on this saved time for writing, and you can't think of one thing to write, write across the top of a page, or type on your computer screen, "I can't think of anything to write." Keep doing that, over and over again. I've done it—and I usually think of something to write after writing, "I can't think of anything to write" several times.

3. Avoid distractions, especially those you create for yourself. How easy it is, in the middle of a writing session, to check your email, or look to see what's going on with your Facebook friends. I have this problem, and I know other writers do as well. What I do is compromise—I will only look at my emails once an hour. Another distraction that writers often create for themselves, to avoid actually writing, is to make sure their desk is neat and tidy. I've gotten over this—my desk is a mess; there are papers and books piled here and there and everywhere. And it doesn't matter.

4. Don't let deadlines and promises create anxiety. Try to remain relaxed and work at a moderate pace. Be careful with promises. For instance, two weeks before a family reunion, I would suggest you not promise to have an in-depth story written about Uncle Jake who ran off with the local school teacher back in 1930 and made a name for himself—but not the kind of name most people know about.

5. Realize that what you are writing is a first draft, not a final product. Trying to write everything perfectly the first time blocks many writers. They fuss over whether words are spelled correctly, whether the commas are in the right place, and whether everything makes sense. As a result, they accomplish little as they write and rewrite their first paragraphs or sometimes even their first sentences. It took me awhile to realize that I can't—indeed, I don't know if any writers could (although there may be one or two)—create their best effort the first time through. See chapter 11 where I talk about rewriting and its importance.

The Creating Self and the Judging Self

We each have within us a creative self and a judging self. For most of us, the judging self is better developed—it's the part of us that looks over our shoulder at everything we do and makes some comment about it. This is especially true in writing, when the judging self examines every word, every sentence, and every paragraph we write and usually has something negative to say about it. Here's one solution to the problem: When you begin writing a story, keep going. Don't stop to correct things, but forge on. Later, you can come back and make the necessary corrections. By doing this, you are allowing your creative self to take over, to ply your memory and sift out the stories that reside there—and put them down on paper.

A technique I suggest to students who are challenged by their judging self is to do "timed writing." I tell them to pick a topic, set their kitchen timer for ten or fifteen minutes, and then begin writing and continue writing without stopping to change or correct anything until the timer rings. Timed writing allows your creative self to come out and play, while your judging self is frustrated because you don't pause long enough for it to kick in and give you grief.

Misguided Perfection

Several years ago a writing student in my workshop was working on the first paragraph of what she said would be a series of her life stories. "I want this first paragraph to be perfect before I move on," she said. Unfortunately, she never got past the first paragraph. She wrote and re-wrote it. I suggested to her that she set the first paragraph aside and move on. But she didn't. I didn't have the heart to tell her that in a later revision and rewrite of the completed story, what she had as a first paragraph could be dropped.

The following year she returned to the writing workshop. I assumed she had written several stories and asked if she would be sharing them with the workshop participants. She said, incredibly, "No, I'm still working on making that first long paragraph perfect." I never did figure out if she was the ultimate procrastinator, really didn't want to write her life stories, or indeed was caught up in misguided perfection.

What I do, and what I suggest my students do, is write a story all the way through, even though it may take several days or more to do it. Write without worrying about spelling, grammar, or punctuation. Just write, as quickly as you can, for what you are doing is capturing the essence of the story you are writing. In chapter 11, I will talk about how to rewrite and revise the story. Revising a story while you are in the midst of it almost never works.

Waiting for the Muse

You've likely heard about the "muse." You may have even said, during one of your moments of procrastination, "I really can't work on my story until I hear from the muse." Occasionally I hear one of my writing students using the muse excuse for not getting at their writing.

So what is the muse? One dictionary definition says, "A muse is a spirit or source that inspires an artist." I suspect we'd all benefit from having the muse visit us from time to time, and the more often the better. As a professional writer I try to write every day, at least five days a week. Some days the writing comes easily, the words fly up to the computer screen—truly the muse is on my shoulder guiding my way, giving me the inspiration and energy to create and create more. Then there are other days, when each word, each sentence, each paragraph is work, hard work. I struggle to find the right word. I agonize because nothing seems to be going well. When I go back to this writing, sometimes a week or two later, I discover something interesting. I expect to find that the writing when the muse was present—or at least seemed to be present—would be much better than the writing I did when the muse was off visiting someone else. However, easy-come writing and agonizingly difficult writing, when compared on a quality basis, are exactly the same. My conclusion: Keep on writing. Some days it will be fun; some days not so much. But the writing will not differ, at least not for me it doesn't. The important thing is getting the story down.

Free Writing

One way to start a story is do what is called free writing. Free writing allows your creative self to come out and play, while your judging self stays frustrated behind the scenes because you don't pause long enough for it to kick in and give you grief.

Select a story idea you want to write about, perhaps a story about your favorite toy when you were a child or a story about something someone did for you that made a difference in your life. Set your kitchen timer for ten minutes, and write nonstop until the bell rings.

Here are some additional prompts for free writing exercises:

- Finish the sentence: "I used to think…"
- Answer the question: "What was the worst job you ever had?"
- Write about three people who made a difference in your life and why.
- Jot down five things that annoy you. Write a story about one of them.

- Write a description of yourself as if someone else were writing it.
- What was the first time you were afraid?
- What could you live without?
- What could you not live without?
- Write for five minutes about each of the following;
  - The color green
  - The smell of freshly baked bread
  - The sound of thunder
  - When you were lonely
  - Silence.

Many people find free writing, sometimes referred to as timed or forced writing, to be creative, surprising, often revealing, and a fun activity. But it's not for everyone. You'll have to decide if it works for you.

Six-word Story

An interesting exercise is to write about something that happened in your life in six words. By doing so, you make every word count. It's a way of getting to the nub of your story without beating around the bush with extra, sometimes distracting material. Ernest Hemingway is credited with the following six-word story: "For Sale: Baby shoes, never worn." As a child I had polio. One of my six-word stories is: "Polio at twelve. Still limping today."

I use this exercise in my writing workshops, and generally get two kinds of reactions: "Oh, this is easy. Shouldn't take any time at all to write several of these," or "This seems extremely difficult; I don't think I can do it."

For some, it does appear easy to do. The six words seem to appear on paper with little difficulty, but for most, even those who thought it seemed absurdly easy, they find it a challenge to find exactly the right six words to make a story.

Some life-story writers begin with a six-word story and then expand it into a much longer story—the six-word story helps to keep them focused as they develop the more complex and complete story. Others write their story, and then try to create a six-word story that captures the essence of the longer story they have written.

Almost all participants in my workshops find the six-word story interesting and for some, a welcome break from writing longer pieces. The six-word story, however it is viewed, makes the important point that each word counts in a story—and conversely, stories often can be strengthened when words are eliminated—when "less is more."

11

Revising and Rewriting

For 32 years I taught creative writing at the School of the Arts in Rhine-lander, Wisconsin. In addition to writing workshops, the school offered painting, dance, music, woodcarving, and other art-related workshops. One day I stopped by the woodcarver's room to see what he was doing and to chat for a bit. One of his specialties was carving wooden wild ducks.

"How do you go about carving a duck?" I asked him. His quick answer was, "You start with a block of wood and then you go looking for a duck." He meant of course that he carved away everything that did not contribute to the final product he was looking for.

"Do you always find a duck?" I asked, smiling.

"Nope, I don't. I have lots of kindling for my wood stove, though."

I thought about that exchange many times and concluded that writing our stories is very much like carving a duck. He starts with a block of wood; we start with an empty computer screen or a blank sheet of paper. His first attempt usually results in something that looks like a duck, but only a rough approximation. Our first draft probably looks like the story we want to tell—but, like the woodcarver—it requires lots of additional work. The duck carver whittles away, removing extraneous wood, shaping, forming, creating the feathers in the wings, forming the tail just right, and shaping the head so it's realistic.

We work with our story, removing excessive adjectives and adverbs, sharpening the beginning, creating an interesting middle, and a satisfying end. Different from the woodcarver, we can add additional words if necessary and we can also move pieces of our story around—what we have as an ending may better work as the beginning. The woodcarver can't do that, and thus he sometimes ends up with kindling wood. We end up with drafts, many drafts, until our story is just right. The head looks realistic, the wings look like they could fly, and the body looks like it will float.

I generally spend more time revising and rewriting than I do creating the first draft of a story—sometimes twice as much time. Here is the process I follow, but you will need to work out a process that works best for you.

Ideas for Rewriting and Revising

Write Entire Story with No Correcting

I try to write the story I am working on all the way through, even though it's sometimes a struggle. Usually I find a certain momentum developing as I force myself to keep going, but not always. There is also a practical reason, especially for those of us who believe rewriting and revision is essential for doing quality work—if you don't have a rough draft of the entire story, you have nothing to revise and rewrite. You need to have it all in front of you before you can do serious revising and rewriting.

While it may sound like a contradiction to what I said above, there is the occasional writing student will do some minor revising as she or he works on a story, and it doesn't get in the way of their storytelling. Some of these students tell me that as a warm-up to their writing, they do some minor revising of the work they had just previously done. It reminds them of where they are in the story, get the writing juices flowing, and seems to help them in creating the reminder of the story they are working on.

Allow the Story to Rest

I usually am elated when I finish the first draft of a story. And sometimes, incorrectly, I believe that this first draft is perfect and there is no possible way that it could be improved, and thus no writing or rewriting is necessary. It's certainly okay to celebrate and feel good about finishing the first draft of a story. I do it. But to believe that the piece requires no further work is a major error. I've known only a handful of people who can write well-developed, carefully crafted stories in first draft.

I usually work on two or three and sometimes even four writing projects at the same time. Thus when I've finished one story, I allow it to rest for at least a couple weeks and sometimes a month, while I turn to work on another one. As someone who grew up making and eating lots of sauerkraut—a fermented product—I tell my writing students the importance of letting their newly created stories ferment. By setting the story aside, you come back to it with fresh eyes.

During this fermentation stage, my subconscious has been working on the story without my knowing it. I discover this when I find the story and read it again.

Read the Entire Story and Then Ask,
"What is This Story About?"

After the resting time, read your story all the way through. While reading, I don't stop to make any changes, but I keep on reading. With fresh eyes, I usually spot a number of errors, both small and large. I make a little check-mark by the error, but I keep going. When I have finished I ask, "What is this story about?" I try to answer the question in a sentence or two. If it takes more than a couple of sentences to say what the story is about, a red flag goes up in my mind.

Before I go on, here is a lesson I learned more than forty years ago, when I was beginning to write books. I had completed a manuscript for a book and sent it to a New York publisher, who indicated interest in the project. He asked if I would be able to fly out to New York and meet with him in his Manhattan office to discuss the book. I invested $238.00 (the round-trip airfare from Madison, Wisconsin to New York), got reservations at the then-famous Algonquin Hotel, and flew off to the big city, filled with excitement and anticipation.

I stayed the night at the Algonquin, expecting to meet a famous author or two—no such luck—and appeared the following morning at the publisher's offices. I cooled my heels in the waiting room for a half hour or so, and then the publisher appeared. He was a tall, lanky, middle-aged man and after he shook my hand, he pointed my way toward his office. When we arrived in his office, he picked up my manuscript, which sat on a chair near him. After a couple inquiries about my trip to New York, he tapped on my manuscript, which he now held on his lap.

"Tell me what this book is about," he said.

I thanked him for asking and proceeding to talk about the book. After a minute or so, he interrupted. "Can you tell me in a sentence or two what your book is about?"

I was taken aback by his question, as I'd thought the minute or so explanation that I had just given had answered his first instruction quite well. I didn't say anything. Then he looked me right in the eye and said, "If you can't tell me what your book is about in a sentence or two, you don't know what it's about." He handed the manuscript back to me. "Why don't you go back to Madison, figure out what your book is about, and get back in touch with me."

I was crushed. I had high hopes of landing a New York publisher for the work, and now all I got out of the trip to the Big Apple was some words of advice. But I have never forgotten the words, and although it cost me well over $350.00, with hotel and taxi costs—a lot of money for a budding author in the 1970s—it turned out to be money well spent. The question of what the story is about centers on theme and focus.

Now, after reading a new story I've written, I write a sentence or two on what I believe the story is about and I place it alongside my computer. The answer guides my rewrite and revision. (By the way, the New York publisher did not publish my work, but another publisher did, after I'd done considerable rewriting).

Once I have written down what the story is about, I re-read the story once more, and everything that does not contribute to "what the story is about" I remove. Often I will also find weak spots, where I must add more to my story.

Are the Scenes in the Proper Order?

Are the story's scenes in the proper order so that the story makes sense; or do I need to rearrange them so the point of the story is clear and unambiguous? Does a scene at the end of the story more properly belong at the beginning? Have I given away the punch line for a humorous scene too soon? Does moving a few scenes around help to create more suspense, and so on?

A Compelling Beginning

I've long been interested in first lines and how they capture attention. Here are some familiar examples from famous novels.

"Call me Ishmael." — Herman Melville, *Moby Dick.*

"It was a bright cold day in April, and the clocks were striking thirteen."—George Orwell, *1984.*

"It was the best of times, it was the worst of time, it was the age of wisdom, it was the age of foolishness, it was the epoch of belief, it was the epoch of incredulity, it was the season of light it was the season of darkness, it was the spring of hope, it was the winter of despair."—Charles Dickens, *A Tale of Two Cities.*

Here are examples of opening sentences from nonfiction books I have on my shelf:

"When I wrote the following pages, or rather the bulk of them, I lived alone, in the woods, a mile from any neighbor, in a house I had built myself, on the shore of Walden Pond."—Henry David Thoreau, *Walden.*

"When I was a boy in Scotland I was fond of everything that was wild, and all my life I've been growing fonder and fonder of wild places and wild creatures."—John Muir, *The Story of my Boyhood and Youth.*

"At the age of eighty my mother had her last bad fall, and after that her mind wandered free through time."—Russell Baker, *Growing Up.*

For my own memoir, *Limping Through Life: A Farm Boy's Polio Memoir,* I wrote: "It came in the night, unannounced and unexpected."[21]

I will sometimes revise and rewrite the first sentence and first paragraph of a story ten times or more. This almost sounds absurd, but I want the beginning of my story to read like I had just written it right off the top of my head. The reality is that making the beginning appear that way often requires lots of rewriting.

Rhythm in the Writing

To check for rhythm in my writing, I read the story aloud, listening for how the words flow or do not flow together. To say it in a way that many of us remember, I search for sentences and phrases that, when read aloud, sound like a fingernail scratching on a blackboard—these I change. One way to check rhythm is to read your story into a recorder, then play it back, listening to the words you are reading as you follow along with the manuscript. By the way, reading aloud and then listening to the recording of your story is another great way to discover omitted words, inappropriate word choices, and sentences that need repair. (See chapter 9 for more about rhythm and why it's important in your writing.)

Check Punctuation, Grammar, and Spelling

Unfortunately, some writers believe this is the sum total of what revising and rewriting is all about. It is an important step to be sure, but is one of the last steps in my rewriting/revising process.

Word processor programs offer tools such as "spell check" that can help you spot spelling errors. But be careful: words that sound alike but have different meanings such as *to*, *two*, and *too* need a careful checking with human eyes to make sure they are used properly. Microsoft Word, the program I use for writing, also has a grammar checker that can be helpful, but it is not foolproof. I still rely on my basic knowledge of grammar that I learned so many years ago in elementary school. *The Elements of Style* by Strunk and White book is also a big help with grammar and usage questions.

All of my commercially published writing is read and corrected by copy editors who are trained to find spelling, grammar, and punctuation errors. My advice to those writing stories as a record for their family or to file with their local library or historical society is to consider hiring a professional editor. An editor will spot obvious errors and likely will also provide feedback on the story itself and make suggestions for improvement. But be careful in answering ads for professional editors. Be sure to get references and know upfront what the professional editor will do for you and at what cost.

Ask Others to Read Your Story

Having others read your story can help improve it. But you must be careful about whom you ask to do it, and don't share it until you have completed the revising and rewriting steps. The tendency for those who are married or have partners is to share the story with your partner. Generally it is not a good idea because you are putting your partner in a difficult spot. He or she is faced with saying, "Oh, this is such a wonderful story, and so well written, too," (which might be the ultimate white lie). Or your partner may say, "Let me show you where you can make this a better story." Often this is a gentle way for your spouse to tell you the piece really isn't that good and requires more work. The "wonderful" comment is of no help for the rewrite/revision process, but does make you feel good. The "this needs work" comment can lead to some difficult partner discussion and a bunch of defensive statements on the part of the author. So generally it is best to avoid your partner as a reader.

For me, I am fortunate that my daughter Susan, who is a published author and who has a graduate degree in reading, reads my stories and usually has many ideas for improvement—especially in the areas of "Dad, this doesn't make sense," to "Exactly what are you trying to say here?" My daughter-in-law is the managing editor of a regional magazine. She reads my material from the perspective of "Will readers understand what I am saying?" She is also wonderful in finding technical errors—grammar, punctuation, spelling, and elusive typos. Finally, in a contradiction of what I said above, my wife, Ruth, reads all of my material. She has a degree in English, has a great eye for finding errors both small and large, and has worked with my writing for as long as we've been married.

Writers' Groups

Writing is a lonely task. We do it by ourselves; most of us like to be alone when we are writing, with as few disturbances as possible. But, as I suggest above, sharing your writing with other people can help you improve what you are writing, even though it may seem painful at the time. In addition to sharing with one or two other people, many writers, especially beginning writers, discover that joining a writing group can be helpful.

Check with your local librarian or bookstore owner and you'll likely discover that there are one or more writers' groups in your community. You'll want to do a little discreet checking before joining one—you want to make sure that the writing group is one that fits you. Get in touch with a couple members of the group, find out what they do, and quietly learn if they are serious writers or simply enjoying getting together as a social outlet. There's nothing wrong with socializing, of course, but as a beginning story writer, you are first looking for feedback on your writing and suggestions for improving it. The better writing groups have several rules, including expecting serious writing, being prepared to read aloud to the group, and accepting criticism without becoming defensive. For most writers, one of the greatest values from belonging to a writing group is hearing the reactions to your writing from others, in addition to gaining valuable suggestions for how to make your writing better.

A couple years ago I had the privilege of working with a writing group in Park Falls, Wisconsin. The group, consisting of fifteen members, meets Mondays from 5:30 to 7 p.m. in the boardroom of the public library, which is on the third floor. They call themselves the Third Story Writer's Guild, and they have been meeting since 2009. Karen, the group's facilitator, explains:

> As Guild's facilitator it is my belief writers need to commune with other writers. People who are not writers do not often understand what makes us tick. We have a commonality, even if we write in different genres, that only other writers seem to grasp. Thus we band together with folks who "get it." [22]

At each meeting, the group does some writing—often freestyle writing, which Karen explains this way:

> We do much in the area of free-writing. A writing prompt, visual or written, is thrown out and members have a set amount of time to expound on it. Free writing engages the creative process in a spontaneous way, often opening a floodgate to something new, exciting, and different. [23]

The group also does a considerable amount of critiquing of each other's work. Peg said that she enjoys the immediate feedback when she reads a chapter from her book. She says the critiques "spark questions, illuminate language, and help [her] to catch errors in time, place, and characterization." She never feels she is "flying solo"—her fellow writers help lift her over the "rough stuff." [24]

Anna Marie said this about the importance of the group:

We each bring something to the table—literally and figuratively—each Monday night. I joined the group looking for feedback and tips on writing and found instead the camaraderie of talented word smiths, the humor and no-nonsense approach of Midwest folks, and a love of the written word to equal my own.[25]

It's also helpful, and many writer groups do this, to have group members read the story prior to a meeting and make written comments to be given to the author of the story. The written comments should include the strong points as well as suggestions for improving the story. There are some dangers in doing this. Often there will be disagreement among the group members, and you will receive contradictory advice about how to improve your story. Occasionally a group member will offer an entirely new way of writing the story—sometimes reflecting how this person would handle the topic—and not necessarily a suggestion that will help you improve what you have written. When this happens, you must always remember that the story is yours. Once the critique session is finished and you are back home, after reviewing the written comments, and the notes you've taken from the oral discussion, you need to decide which suggestions you will follow and which you will ignore.

Writers' groups are not for everyone. I remember after I'd been writing for several years and had several publishing successes, I was feeling a bit noncreative and, to be honest, stuck. I decided that a writing group might be just the thing to jumpstart my writing. I selected four writing friends, all professional writers, and asked if they'd like to be a part of a writing group where we would read one another's writing, offer criticism, and help one another along. "Besides," I told them, "wouldn't it be fun to get together every couple of weeks for a beer and some discussion?" They agreed.

All four of these friends had published books. One was also a full-time daily newspaper columnist. One was a pastor, and one worked for a nonprofit organization. Our little group fizzled after the first meeting. It took me a while to figure out why. We each had our own way of doing things, and our egos were too big to accept much criticism from our peers. I suspect that in some way, although we were friends, we also saw ourselves as competitors.

Guidelines for a successful writer' group include: check your ego at the door; agree to read, write, share, and compare; and be open to criticism—after all, improving your writing is your goal when joining a writers' group.

Email Buddies

Having an email buddy is another technique for gaining feedback for your writing, and one that I suggest to members of my writing workshops. I suggest that as students listen to the writing of others in the workshop, they select someone who is at about the same level as they are, and work out an arrangement that they will read and comment on the other person's writing and in turn should expect that person to do the same for their writing. Sometimes a trio can be involved in email sharing, but more than that and the process becomes unwieldy. The important point is for our stories to be the best they can possibly be, and feedback from other people can be of tremendous help.

PART IV

Telling Your Story Beyond the Page

12

Speaking to a Live Audience

Before you think about telling your story to an audience, you should write it down. I recommend this for several reasons. By writing your story you are creating a written record—a historical document that can be shared with family, filed at a local historical society or perhaps a public library, or in some instances published so that a wider audience can read your story. Of course, writing your story provides all the power and benefits that I discussed earlier: discovering meaning in your life, examining your past while giving you confidence for the future, tying your generation to those that follow, sharing a bit of who you really are, and taking you to a place where you have never been.

And practically speaking, once you have written your story, you are better prepared to share it with a live audience, on the radio, and on television.

Telling your story to a live audience is exciting and satisfying, but for some it can be a terrifying experience. Some friends tell me that they are simply not cut out for public speaking, and they try to avoid doing it whenever they can. When they do find themselves in front of an audience, their mouth goes dry, they begin to perspire, their knees and hands shake, their stomach is in knots—and in the most serious cases, they have what amounts to a panic attack.

Some writer friends I know say they are solitary people, enjoy being by themselves, do their best writing when no one else is around, and simply can't wrap their minds around standing and talking in front of thirty or forty or more people.

I must confess that I was one of those people. I hated crowds—still do—and when asked to speak in front of a group larger than a dozen or so, I was uncomfortable. But I learned to get over it, and in fact even enjoy it as I now often speak to crowds of 300 or more.

I grew up a shy little farm boy who enjoyed being alone. When a stranger drove into our farmyard, I would hide in the woods behind our house until they left. This of course exasperated my mother, as she was prone to "show off" her little boys to whomever might come by.

I started first grade at our one-room country school shortly after I turned five years old. As the fall term got underway, I learned from my teacher that I should plan to "say my piece" at the annual Christmas Program. She told me this shortly after Thanksgiving break, when the entire school (all eight grades in one room) began preparing for this major event in the school. It was an event that everyone in the community attended, whether they had children in school or not. I told the teacher—as a five year old I don't know where I got the gumption to do it—that I didn't want to "say my piece" on stage and that I hated crowds and surely couldn't stand up and speak in front of one. She would buy none of my argument, but she did say she had a secret that I might find useful and that it would help me avoid stage fright, words that I didn't quite understand at the time.

It took a while before she got around to sharing "the secret" with me, as I fretted about standing in front of a group in my new bib overalls and flannel shirt and making a fool of myself—or so I thought.

"Are you still worried about standing on the stage and saying your piece?" she asked a few days later.

"I am. I'm worried sick about it."

"No need to worry," she said, as she sat me down near her desk in the front of the schoolroom. In a soft voice she said, "Do you see that damper on the stove pipe in the back of the room?" Our schoolroom was heated with a wood stove.

"Yes, I see the damper," I replied, wondering what a stove damper had to do with saying my piece in a schoolroom filled with friends, relatives, and neighbors.

"Here's what you do," she said in a near whisper. "When you stand on the stage, don't look at the audience, but look at that damper in the back of the room. The audience will think you are looking right at them, but you are not."

That was an important lesson for a five year old frightened out of his britches at the thought of talking to a roomful of people. I did what she said, and everything worked out fine. When people today ask about my early speaking experience, I tell them this story, and I often say that I've spent my entire career speaking to groups and looking "at the damper in back of the room." Of course it's not true, but for those just getting started, it's one way to allay the jitters that can go when telling your story in front of a room full of people.

Pluses and Minuses

When you write your story, the reader has nothing to go on but your words and how you string them together into a story. But when you are speaking, you have the words but you also have your voice, which you can vary in tone and inflection; your facial expressions and of course the gestures you offer with your hands and arms. These are powerful adjuncts to the words.

On the other hand, there are several disadvantages that can occur when presenting your work. If an audience member misses a point, a phrase, or an important word in your story, he or she cannot go back to see what it was. If people don't "get it" the first time, they simply don't get it. (A question and answer period after your talk can help solve this problem.) Another disadvantage is time constraints. You will often have more story to tell than time allows.

Shortly after my book *Limping Through Life* (about my experience with polio) came out, I was asked to speak to a Rotary Club, where I was limited to 30 minutes. I had given some form of the talk to several other groups, but I'd usually had up to an hour to speak. I made my story fit the 30-minute limit, but I felt I had to leave out some important components. I am slowly learning how to share my stories within the time constraints that I have—especially when I am talking on live radio and TV.

Sometimes I also find myself in a room with seventy-five people and no microphone or an inadequate microphone, meaning a goodly number of people can't hear what I have to say. There is nothing more aggravating to both speaker and audience than a situation where the audience can't hear you. Thankfully I have a strong voice, and after many years of teaching, I have learned how to project it.

Tips for Storytelling to a Live Audience

Don't Read Your Story

Do not read the story you have written to an audience. And don't feel you should memorize the story you have written and then recite it. Having worked long and hard on your story, after excavating the background research and perhaps interviewing several people, and then after writing and rewriting the text—probably several times—you know your story. You may not remember it word for written word, and it is not expected that you should. Sharing your story spontaneously has great power, beyond the fact that you are freed from the written page. You can look at your audience, use hand gestures, and include all the tricks used by good public speakers.

From time to time, you might read a short quotation or a paragraph from the written story to help amplify your presentation—but here is another example of where less is more. The less reading you do the better.

For those of you who have had your stories published in a book and are asked to do a reading at a local bookstore, don't read (or at least don't read very much). I one time attended such a "reading." The author, who had published several novels and nonfiction books, was well known and had attracted an audience of a couple hundred people. He is a great writer. He is an awful reader. He droned on for forty-five minutes, seldom looking up from his book, never using any gestures, and with a voice that never varied in pitch or volume. It was like someone had opened a garden hose and the words tumbled out in a constant stream. I wanted more—I could read the story on my own. I wanted a little excitement. I wanted to be drawn into the story, not sit quietly listening as a distant bystander.

Keep Your Listeners Engaged

A trick I've learned that keeps audience members engaged is to ask them questions during my presentation. If I am talking about one of my books on rural life, I will break the ice by asking, "How many of you grew up on a farm?" I ask for a show of hands. I usually ask two follow-up questions: "How many of you have had some relationship to a farm or farming?" and finally, "How many of you have driven by a farm?" The last question always draws a little laughter.

Use of Visuals

Use of visuals in your storytelling can help, but it can also get in the way of your story. When I talk to schoolchildren about what it was like to grow up without electricity, I often bring along a barn lantern similar to the kind I used when I was a kid on the farm. Then I tell stories about doing farm chores by lantern light, and doing our school homework by lamplight. The lantern helps make the stories more real.

A few years ago, I wrote a children's book about how one year we grew three acres of rutabagas on the home farm and while it was a fine crop, we had difficulty selling them. When I shared the story with children's groups, I brought along several rutabagas. We had whole ones and some that we sliced into small pieces so the children could taste them. As I told the story, I passed the whole rutabagas around so the students could feel them, and then the samples so they could taste them as well. Having the real thing—some actual rutabagas—made the story come alive.

I wrote a book about my many years of vegetable gardening, including many stories of successes and failures. I've given many talks on this subject, and for these talks I have a Power Point presentation with photos of my garden at various stages during the season. My audience can not only listen, but can also see what I am talking about. But the visuals are there to enhance my stories, not get in the way of them.

More often than not, I tell my stories using no visuals, depending on my voice and gestures. When I talk to audiences about my polio experience (*Limping Through Life*) I use no visuals. Perhaps I am my own visual as I limp to the podium before I share my story.

Tips for Using Visuals

- Visuals should relate to your story. Too many times I have seen speakers flash a visual on the screen—perhaps a cartoon from the newspaper, or a photo—that has absolutely nothing to do with the person's story. When I ask why they do this, they tell me, "Oh, I do this to get the audience's attention." What they have actually done is confuse the audience.

- Make sure everyone in the audience can see the visual. We've all heard speakers say, "I know those of you in the back probably can't see this." Those in the back deserve to see what's on the screen, as much as those sitting in the front row.

- Arrive a little early where you are speaking so you can practice using your visuals, especially if you are using a computer projector. Just recently I saw a speaker who did not check things out ahead of time and discovered that her laptop computer and the projector provided at the meeting site were incompatible. Thankfully, she was a good speaker and got along fine without the visuals.

- Even if you've practiced, be prepared for technical difficulties. When it comes to using computer and audiovisual (AV) systems, if something can go wrong, it will. If this happens to you, don't take forever trying to fix the malfunction; rather, brush it off with a laugh and move on to your Plan B.

- Don't allow your visuals to overpower your story. Too often these days, I see overzealous Power Point creators develop visuals with sounds, flashing lights, and words that jump on and off the screen. Whatever the person's story—and often they don't have one—it is lost in the glitz of visualization.

Practice with a Small Group

For those of you new to oral storytelling, you may want to practice telling your story to a group of friends, and then work your way up to larger audiences.

Service clubs such as Kiwanis, Lions, and Rotary are always looking for programs. They usually want presentations no longer than a half-hour, and there is no payment beyond a free lunch, but it is a great opportunity to gain experience in telling your story out loud.

Some Practical Tips

- Always arrive where you will speak at least a half-hour early. This gives you time to check the sound system and the computer/projector system to make sure they work. It also calms your host's nerves to know that you are there.

- Don't drink cold water before you speak, as it tends to tighten your vocal cords. A sip of warm water or coffee is better.

- Work to avoid saying "You know" or "ah" or whatever else comes out of your mouth when you are thinking about what to say next. As a listener, I have been known to count the number of "you knows" a speaker utters—obviously I am not paying attention to what the speaker has to say because I am so distracted.

- Make sure everyone in the audience can hear, whether you are using a microphone or not. When I begin a presentation, I usually ask, "Can those in the back hear?"

- Even when you use a mic, project your voice. A normal speaking voice, even if you are using a mic, sometimes doesn't make it to the back of the room.

- Don't swallow your words. This means to make sure that you don't mumble or run together words, especially those at the end of sentences.

- Learn to vary the pitch of your voice, sometimes louder, sometimes softer, but always loud enough so everyone can hear.

- When telling a story with several characters in it, practice using different voices for different characters—this technique can give additional life to your stories.

- Use short sentences and simple words. Your purpose is not to impress your audience with your vocabulary, nor with your ability to create long, complicated sentences.

- Try to include some humor in your storytelling.

- As you write your stories with rhythm, tell them with rhythm. Occasionally speak more rapidly, then more slowly, sometimes louder, sometimes with a softer voice.

- Depending on the group and the situation, thirty to forty-five minutes is a good length for a talk, followed by questions and answers. Ask your host ahead of time how long you should talk.

- During the question-and-answer phase, repeat the question before answering it.

- If you don't know the answer to a question, say, "I don't know," rather than stumbling and bumbling together some kind of response.

- Avoid having someone dominate the question and answer period. If this happens, a good response is, "We need to let someone else have a chance."

- If someone challenges you about something you said, perhaps some detail or piece of history shared, say something such as, "That's interesting," or "Thank you for that." Avoid confronting the person.

- Smile. Some speakers look like they are in agony. Perhaps they are, but it's not a good idea to let the audience know it.

- Have fun. If you look and act like speaking to an audience is the last thing you want to be doing, the audience will pick up on it. I've been speaking in front of groups since I was in high school, and I've come to enjoy it. If speaking to an audience is new for you, know that each time you do it, it will become easier and more fun for you.

13

Storytelling on Radio

I have been telling my stories on radio for many years, on commercial stations and on public radio. I've found radio is a powerful way of reaching thousands of people at the same time. I do three types of radio programs. There are those where the interviewer merely wants to talk about my work and perhaps discuss some upcoming event where I am speaking. These are usually short interviews, sometimes only four or five minutes or even less. Generally there is little or no time for storytelling. A second type of program is where the interviewer asks me questions, and because these run a half hour or so, I usually have time to share a story or two. An example is a program I do several times a year for the public radio station in Barrow, Alaska. For each of these programs I share one of my stories.

A third type of radio show I do, which can last forty-five minutes or longer, is a call-in show. I do several of these a year for public radio. The interviewer usually asks me to share a couple of my stories, and then takes questions from listeners. My stories usually prompt listeners to share their stories, so the program becomes non-stop stories. A truly fun experience!

Tips for Doing Radio

With radio, everything depends on your voice and the words you choose to share. It's different from speaking to a live audience, as you have no opportunity to rely on facial expressions and visual aids. Your voice is everything. I asked several long-time radio people to share some tips for telling a story on radio. Mike Crane, the director of Wisconsin Public Radio, said:

Most of all, remember that a story is meant to be told. That is, spoken, not read. We've all heard people on the radio reading their essays, and it sounds like they're completing a class assignment, rather than telling a story. You should think of telling this story to one person, not to "an audience." They're probably listening alone... in the kitchen, in their car... so forget about the fact that thousands may be tuned in, and tell your best friend this story. There's actually a technique we often use that helps this: we'll have a person simply talk to the producer about their story, rather than read it aloud.[26]

Larry Meiller, the long-time host of Wisconsin Public Radio's "The Larry Meiller Show," wrote:

Know what you are talking about! Organize your thoughts and run them through your mind. If you know you will be telling the story, you might make some notes and practice it, but do NOT script it. You want to tell it in your own conversational terms. When you really know your story you will have more fun!

Be interested in what you're saying. It might sound superfluous, but anybody who listens to radio can tell if the speaker is really interested. Enthusiasm is very important... Let the listeners know you really enjoy telling your story![27]

Pam Jahnke, a long-time commercial farm radio broadcaster, offered the following tips:

To me, a good story in radio involves a voice that is clear and commands some attention—a voice that fluctuates with the mood and flow of the story or content you're delivering. A good story should give you enough background to encourage you to keep listening and slowly build to the conclusion. Keep the audience coming along with you through your voice—a pause, a sigh. Theater of the mind.

Personal stories on the radio are wonderful—as long as they don't get too complicated... Quick references, for example, to quirky family members or neighbors that are key to the story are great, but you can't make it too difficult to follow. In today's "need it now" society, you're not afforded the luxury of drawing out too much detail on the radio. You need to set the hook with something that will appeal to a majority of your audience—not your personal pleasure—but the audience's appeal. Reminding yourself all along that not everyone grew up with the same background, life experiences, or education is critical. Then use your voice, your language/descriptions, to keep your personal reference in place but advance the story. And by all means HAVE A POINT! A story that's told with no point or goal is a waste of radio airtime—and people only generally give you one chance.[28]

A Good Story for Radio

A good story for radio is not too different from a good story told in writing, in person, or on television. Larry Meiller also offered some suggestions about what makes a good story for radio:

A good story typically has a bit of tension and it has an arc. You want people's attention right away so you have an opening sentence that will grab their attention. Start with something that conveys action. Here's a wild example but it is one I actually heard:

"It all started when Don Jackson's toilet blew up." There's no way you would not listen to that story! Then you have the body of the story and finally the conclusion. Conclusions are important and you should not meander. It's nice to have a sentence or two that wraps up the story.[29]

Here are some additional tips for telling your story on radio:

- Be conversational. Speak as if you are telling your story to a friend. Use words you use in everyday conversation. Avoid trying to impress listeners with your vast vocabulary.

- Avoid complicated, long sentences. Avoid saying, "Joe Smith, long-time farmer and active in his community, had a dark side most people did not know about." Better to say, "Joe Smith was a long-time farmer and active in his community. He had a dark side most people did not know about."

- Remember that you are telling a story, not reciting a series of facts. Go beyond the facts. Help your listeners know that your story matters, and that it may include some lesson to be learned.

- Help listeners "see" what you are saying by describing people, places, and sounds.

- Be enthusiastic. It's your story; show your excitement about your story in the way in which you share it.

For me, radio is a fun medium for sharing my stories. In recent years, with advances in technology, I do some of my radio programs directly from my home phone; thus I don't even need to travel to a radio station. This also allows me to do programs, such as the one I do in Barrow, Alaska, while sitting at my desk at home—but remembering the three-hour time difference.

14

Appearing on Television

I've found it interesting, exciting, and more than a little challenging to tell my stories on television. I work with both commercial television stations as well as with public television these days. Back in the late 1950s and early 1960s when I worked exclusively with commercial television, there were no retakes. TV was live and what happened at the moment went on the air for all to view. In the early 1960s, I worked for the University of Wisconsin as an extension agent, working with farmers in Brown County (Green Bay, Wisconsin). Three commercial TV stations were on the air in Green Bay at the time, and I had many opportunities to tell stories about agriculture in the area.

Each fall, the counties in northeastern Wisconsin sponsored a live-stock show for the 4-H and FFA (Future Farmers of America) members in the area. One of the local stations asked me to do a program about the livestock show, and if possible bring in a live animal. I chose a young 4-H member and her prize lamb. I was told to fill about 15 or 20 minutes, so I had lots of time to interview the young woman and get the story about her lamb.

Alice in Dairyland was also supposed to be a part of the show, but she had not yet arrived at the station when the show began. When she arrived, she was wearing a full-length gown with a corsage pinned to the top left side. Alice apparently had little experience with lambs. After we greeted each other, and I introduced her to the young woman I was interviewing, she bent over to pet the lamb saying, "Oh, what a cute little lamb." The lamb then took a huge bite out of Alice's corsage. Her face turned red as she pulled back, grasping her gown that had sagged a bit.

And I, startled as she was, blurted out, "That little lamb sure has good taste."

The entire floor staff burst into laughter, and the show went to a commercial. I did many more live programs at that station, but the station manager told me that nothing garnered more audience reaction than the time the lamb embarrassed Alice in Dairyland.

I asked two prominent television people to tell me what makes a good story for television, as well as offer some tips for those telling the stories.

Stories for Television

Jon Miskowski, Development Director of Wisconsin Television, suggested the following:

> *A good story has tension.* Antiques Roadshow *is an example of a highly successful TV show. It's hard to turn away from it because it captures the viewer. The program has the traditional story arc—you want to know how every story turns out. Great example of story after story. Drama... tension... not simply the revealing of a price. People watch for the price, but viewers are interested in how this plays out for this person. How they got this thing, and what they know about it. If you took those items out of context and said here's this item and what it's worth, people wouldn't watch the show.*

> *A story arc means the story has a beginning, a middle, and an end. The viewer is pulled along. There is a narrative that viewers connect to. A collection of facts from several sources is not a story.*[30]

Mik Derks, an Emmy-winning producer at Wisconsin Public Television, said this when I asked, "What makes a good story for television?":

> *I am looking for the passion, for the emotion, for what people are feeling about an experience. Stories have a beginning, a middle, and an end. The viewer loves the truth. That goes back to why the firsthand account is so important—there is no interpretation. You are telling what happened; there may be some interpretation in what it meant to you. People respond to that truth. What they are hearing is a glimpse of the past. When a veteran shares war stories, the person next door can better relate to these personal stories than those told by a general, or a historian, or a reporter. As a viewer, it is easier for you to put yourself in the storyteller's place because the story is coming*

from a regular person. You can put yourself in their place and vicariously decide how you would respond in a situation like that. Many stories on TV are far away from life as we recognize it. People are attracted to documentaries for that reason.[31]

Tips for Telling Stories on Television

Mik Derks offers these suggestions for telling stories as part of a TV documentary:

> *Some people want to read their stories on TV—not the way to go. When someone gets a date wrong, we can fix that. I'm not going to put you out there and make you look like a liar or look stupid. People are their story and should trust themselves to tell their story. Just let it flow.*
>
> *Three words of advice for an interviewee:*
> **There are no wrong answers.** *Whatever someone asks you, you're the one who knows the answer. Don't worry about giving what the interviewer wants to hear.*
>
> **Don't get hung up on getting the details exactly right.**
> *Details are important because they bring the past to life. But don't spend five minutes worrying about if something happened before or after you graduated from high school.*
>
> **Don't self-edit as you are speaking, spending too much time trying to pick the right word.** *You must be comfortable—if you are self-editing you may very well forget the essence of the story you are trying to tell.*
>
> *The hardest thing in the world is to tell a person to relax.*[32]

I do two very different types of television shows. Occasionally I am asked to appear on a commercial television station for a brief interview about one of my books. Usually I only have a few minutes of time, so in addition to answering questions, I may have time for a very brief story. I know this ahead of time, and I have ready a minute-long or even shorter story. This sounds challenging for those accustomed to giving half-hour or longer story-telling performances. But think about the hundreds of story-telling TV commercials that are sometimes only 30 seconds long, and yet they tell a story.

Most of the television work I do these days is with public television, where I have been fortunate to participate in creating hour-long documentaries. Doing these shows, there is ample time to tell stories, short and long. But even so, they must follow all the guidelines for a good story or they will fall flat.

Of course with TV, different from radio, not only can you use your voice, but your facial expressions, and other gestures can be a part of the story. Visuals, film clips, and still photography can be part of the presentation as well.

Both TV and radio storytelling can be demanding, as our audience these days, in its zeal to do everything more quickly, is often prone to have a short attention span. All the more reason to make sure our stories are the best they can possibly be, and presented to the best of our abilities.

Telling your story, which is one of the most interesting and worthwhile things a person can do, begins with a written story. It can then be shared in written form, shared in person with a live audience, and additionally shared on radio and TV. Although writing the story can be of great benefit to the writer, sharing the story can also help others. Although sometimes a bit challenging, every step of the process—from coming up with a story idea to sharing it with others—can be one of the most fun things a person can do.

It's never too late to get started—time to get busy.

Notes

1. Alter, Adam. *Drunk Tank Pink*. New York, New York: The Penguin Press, 2013, p. 4.

2. Goldberg, Natalie. *Old Friend from Far Away*. New York, New York: Free Press, 2007, p. xviii.

3. Lamb, Nancy. *The Art and Craft of Storytelling*. Cincinnati, Ohio: Writer's Digest Books, 2008, p. 5.

4. Martin, Phillip. "What is a Story?" http://janefriedman. com/2011/09/27/what-is-a-story/

5. Zinsser, William. *Writing About Your Life*. New York, New York: Marlowe & Company, 2004, p. 29.

6. Personal Interview with Jon Miskowski, Development Director, Wisconsin Public Television, 3/2/14.

7. Rico, Gabriele Lusser. *Writing the Natural Way*. Los Angeles: J. P. Tarcher, 1981, p. 29.

8. Apps, Jerry. *Every Farm Tells a Story*. St. Paul, Minnesota: Voyageur Press, 2005, pp. 68–70.

9. Interview with Mik Derks, 2/21/14.

10. Apps, Jerry. *Living a County Year*. St. Paul, Minnesota: Voyageur Press, 2007, p.31.

11. Apps, Jerry. *Every Farm Tells a Story*. St. Paul, Minnesota: Voyageur Press, 2005, pp. 156–157.

12. Lamb, Nancy. *The Art and Craft of Storytelling*. Cincinnati, Ohio: Writer's Digest Books, 2008, pp. 121–123.

13. Interview with Mik Derks, 2/21/14.

14. Barrington, Judith. *Writing the Memoir*. Portland, Oregon: The Eighth Mountain Press, 1997, p. 109.

15. Apps, Jerry. *Whispers and Shadows*. Madison, Wisconsin: Wisconsin Historical Society Press, 2015, pp. 81–83.

16. Apps, Jerry. *Living a County Year*. St. Paul, Minnesota: Voyageur Press, 2007, p.31.

17. Larson, Olaf F. *When Horses Pulled the Plow*. Madison, Wisconsin: University of Wisconsin Press, 2011.

18. Apps, Jerry. *Every Farm Tells a Story*. Minneapolis, Minnesota: Voyageur Press, 2005, pp. 151–153.

19. Apps, Jerry. *The Quiet Season: Remembering Country Winters*. Madison, Wisconsin: Wisconsin Historical Society Press, 2013, pp. 64–65

20. Strunk, William Jr., and White, E. B. *The Elements of Style*. Boston, Massachusetts: Allyn and Bacon, 1979, 2000.

21. Apps, Jerry. *Symbols: Viewing a Rural Past*. Amherst, Wisconsin: Amherst Press, 2000, p. 27.

22. Personal correspondence from Karen Dums, March 15, 2013.

23. Ibid.

24. Ibid.

25. Ibid.

26. Email interview with Mike Crane, Director Wisconsin Public Radio. 2/21/2014

27. Email interview with Larry Meiller, 1/29/14.

28. Email interview with Pam Jahnke, "The Farm Report with Pam Jahnke," 2/13/14.

29. Email interview with Larry Meiller, 1/29/14.

30. Personal Interview with Jon Miskowski, Development Director, Wisconsin Public Television, 3/2/14.

31. Interview with Mik Derks, 2/21/14.

32. Interview with Mik Derks, 2/21/14.

References

This reference list is divided into three parts: books that discuss telling your story in writing; books about improving writing skills and journaling; and references about telling your story orally.

Telling Your Story in Writing

1. Barrington, Judith. *Writing the Memoir*. Portland, Oregon: The Eighth Mountain Press, 1997.

   Excellent suggestions for writing a memoir including the statement: "There is more to writing a memoir than simply starting at the beginning and ending at the end."

2. Files, Meg. *Write From Life*. Cincinnati, Ohio: Writer's Digest Books, 2002.

   A good general guide to the process.

3. Goldberg, Natalie. *Old Friend from Far Away: The Practice of Writing Memoir*. New York, New York: Free Press, 2007.

   Everything from inspiration to writing prompts and how walking can assist your storytelling.

4. Hemley, Robin. *Turning Life into Fiction*. St. Paul, Minnesota: Graywolf Press, 2006.

   For those who want to go the second mile and turn one of their life stories into a short story or a novel, Hemley has some suggestions on how to do it. I have done this with several of my stories. See my series of six novels published by the University of Wisconsin Press, and my young adult novel published by Fulcrum Press.

5. Kramer, Mark and Call, Wendy (eds.), *Telling True Stories*. New York: Plume/Penguin, 2007.

   A collection of essays by a variety of storytellers including David Halberstam, Gay Talese, Tracy Kidder, and several others.

6. LaChapelle, Carol. *Finding Your Voice: Telling Your Stories*. Portland, Oregon: Marion Street Press, 2008.

   For those who want to know about telling stories about people, place, and special life experiences.

7. Lamb, Nancy. *The Art and Craft of Storytelling.* Cincinnati, Ohio: Writer's Digest Books, 2008.

"Storytelling is an art. And like any other art, it has rules." This book includes many of them.

8. McCutcheon, Marc, *The Writer's Guide to Everyday Life in the 1800s.* Cincinnati, Ohio: Writer's Digest Books, 1993.

If you are writing about a family member who lived in the 1800s, here you will learn everything from what people wore to how they talked.

9. Maguire, Jack. *The Power of Personal Storytelling: Spinning Tales to Connect With Others.* New York, New York: Tarcher/Putnam, 1998.

Why people tell personal stories, finding story ideas, bringing your story to life, and more.

10. Metzger, Deena, *Writing for Your Life.* New York: Harper Collins, 1992.

Excellent chapter on how story defines our lives. "Every life is a story."

11. Polking, Kirk. *Writing Family Histories and Memoirs.* Cincinnati, Ohio: Betterway Books, 1995.

To tell your story, learning about and telling your family's story often becomes important. Here is a guide for researching and writing about family histories.

12. Rainer, Tristine, *Your Life as Story: Writing the New Autobiography.* New York, New York: Tarcher/Putnam, 1997.

How to examine our lives for stories, and then how to tell them.

.13. Roorbach, Bill. *Writing Life Stories.* Cincinnati, Ohio: Story Press, 1998.

One of the better books on writing your life story. Includes many writing exercises.

14. Stanek, Lou Willett, *Writing Your Story: Putting Your Past on Paper.* New York, New York: Avon Books, 1971.

Giving yourself permission to write your story, focusing, how to show and not tell, and the importance of detail.

15. Zinsser, William. *Writing About Your Life.* New York, New York: Marlowe and Company, 2004.

Zinsser says that the events and people that you write about may not be as important is how the events and the people influenced you.

References for Improving Writing Skills

1. Kidder, Tracy and Todd, Richard. *Good Prose: The Art of Nonfiction.* New York, New York: Random House, 2013.

   About story, character, structure, memoir, facts, and beyond facts.

2. Lamott, Ann. *Bird by Bird.* New York, New York: Doubleday, 1994.

   A classic on how to write, overcoming blocks, the importance of re-writing, and much more.

3. Rico, Gabriele Lusser, *Writing the Natural Way: Using Right-Brain Techniques to Release Your Expressive Powers.* Los Angeles: J. P. Tarcher, 1983.

   For those who want to delve more deeply into mind mapping, from how to do it to what can result from drawing all those circles.

4. Strunk, William, Jr. & White, E. B. *The Elements of Style.* New York, New York: Macmillan, 1979.

   All writers should have this book on their desk. Many words of writing wisdom here.

5. Goldberg, Natalie. *Writing Down The Bones: Freeing the Writer Within.* Boston, Massachusetts: Shambhala, 2010.

   Inspiration, writing tips, excellent book.

6. Lynne Truss. *Eats Shoots & Leaves.* New York, New York: Gotham Books-Penguin Group, 2003.

   A delightful little book on the importance of using punctuation properly. Look how punctuation changes the meaning of these two sentences. "A woman, without her man, is nothing." "A woman: without her, man is nothing."

7. Booth, Wayne; Columb, Gregory; and Williams, Joseph M. *The Craft of Research.* Chicago, Illinois: University of Chicago Press, 2003.

   How to do background research for our storytelling project, and how to include research findings in your work.

Journal Writing

1. Johnson, Alexandra. *On Keeping a Journal, Leaving a Trace: The Art of Transforming a Life into Stories*. New York, New York: Barnes & Noble, 2001.

   Why journaling is important and how to do it. One important reason—triggers memories.

2. Rainer, Tristine, *The New Diary*. New York, New York: Tarcher/Putnam, 1978,

   Rainer writes, "The therapeutic and creative benefits of keeping the New Diary are, in fact, almost as numerous as the people who enjoy the pleasure of keeping it."

Telling Your Story Orally

1. Denning, Stephen. *The Springboard: How Storytelling Ignites Action in Knowledge-Era Organizations*. New York, New York: Routledge, 2011.

   How to use personal storytelling to evoke change.

2. Lipman, Doug. *Improving Your Storytelling: Beyond the Basics for All Who Tell Stories in Work or Play*. Grand Rapids, Michigan: Dickinson Press, 1999.

   Covers your relationship to your listeners, your relationship to the story, and much more.

3. Weissman, Jerry. *Presenting to Win: The Art of Telling Your Story*. Upper Saddle River, New Jersey: FT Press, 2012.

   Everything from communicating visually to bringing your story to life.

Also by Jerry Apps

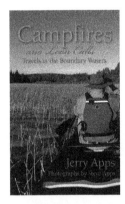

Campfires and Loon Calls:
Travels in the Boundary Waters
978-1-936218-07-3

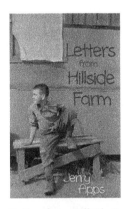

Letters from Hillside Farm
978-1-55591-998-6

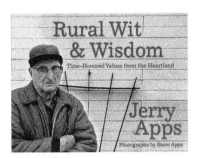

Rural Wit and Wisdom
978-1-55591-601-5

NOTES

NOTES

About the Author

Jerry Apps is Professor Emeritus at the University of Wisconsin–Madison, and the author of more than fifty books, including six novels and five children's books. His most recent novel is *The Great Sand Fracas of Ames County,* and is about sand mining. Some of his recent nonfiction books include *Limping Through Life, The Quiet Season,* and *Whispers and Shadows.*

He has recently completed three hour-long television documentaries about farm life, which aired on PBS nationally.

Jerry's many awards include the Council for Wisconsin Writers' Major Achievement Award in 2007; the Distinguished Service Award from the University of Wisconsin–Madison College of Agricultural and Life Sciences in 2010; selection as Fellow of the Wisconsin Academy of Sciences, Arts and Letters in 2012; and a regional Emmy Award for the television documentary *Farm Winter With Jerry Apps.*